"... when I first stuck my nose into it, I was up to page 80 before I realized lunch had gone cold. ... you come to the last page too soon."

John Leblanc

"... completely winning and thoroughly enjoyable."

Publishers Weekly

"... an absorbing account of a Canadian airman's life in wartime England, as well as the gut-wrenching story of his hours in combat over Occupied Europe."

Harry Flemming, *Atlantic Insight*

"... a wondrously fright-fraught remembrance of times not ready to be forgotten ... all about fear and friendship—and living and dying with some innocently bawdy—and uproarious—stopovers along the way."

Dave Stockand, *Vancouver Sun*

"... hard to put down."

Ernie Lee, *London Free Press*

"... a great story."

A. D. Steubing, *Airforce Magazine*

TERROR IN THE STARBOARD SEAT

TERROR IN THE STARBOARD SEAT

Dave McIntosh

PaperJacks LTD.

Markham, Ontario, Canada

A CANADIAN

PaperJacks

One of a series of Canadian books
published by PaperJacks Ltd.

TERROR IN THE STARBOARD SEAT

PaperJacks edition published December, 1981

ISBN 0-7701-0183-6

For Jean and Sid

CHAPTER ONE

"Up we go," said my uncle and he took me by the armpits and held me so that I was looking down into the coffin at the closed eyelids of my father.

I was seven and he was dead at thirty-five.

Outside, the village street was filled with soldiers, as far as I could see from our living room window past Mr. Meekren's red house on one side and Mr. Labonté's white house on the other. My father had been overseas as a soldier and airman in The Great War, as it was called then, and was president of the Legion's Frontier Branch (Stanstead and Rock Island, Quebec).

He died in November, 1928, and ever since November has been a melancholy month. Christmas was not the big day in our family when I was a boy — November 11, Armistice Day, was. There was a community service in the Opera House and the complete list of "the fallen" was read. It seemed a very long list for just two villages. My heart beat faster until the name Gordon Leslie McIntosh was reached and passed. A wreath was placed on the memorial on Dufferin Heights, the "Last Post" torn away in a scudding sky. Smaller wreaths were placed on each grave marker in Crystal Lake cemetery, footsteps unheard in the grass or on the snow. I wore my father's medals (it was the custom then) and held them against my chest when I ran so they wouldn't clink.

One morning in 1937, I went into the kitchen for breakfast and my mother was sitting at the table reading the *Montreal Gazette* and crying. "You and Robert will have to go to war, just like your father," she said. Robert is my brother.

I looked at the *Gazette*. A royal Yugoslav had been assassinated in Marseille. Sarajevo and Marseille, twenty-three years apart.

My mother was right about the war. She was right about me going, too, but I delayed my enlistment as long as I decently could without incurring a motion of censure from the Frontier Branch. I had heard all those stories about ass-end Charlies (tail gunners) who joined up in haste and were flame-dead over Europe six weeks later.

Nobody ever enlists with the thought that he might be killed. Getting killed is what happens to the other guy. If it weren't that way, nobody would ever volunteer. We all joined up because the other guy did. That's why I did, anyway, though I had a further motive: I had to enlist to be able to graduate from the University of Toronto.

I was busy working my way through college and in 1940 was better off than most married men. I had two jobs and as a result didn't have time to attend lectures in my final year. By the spring of 1942, with exams coming on, I was becoming pretty panicky. How could a failed McIntosh face his mother, let alone his aunts?

Suddenly, Varsity decreed that if you joined up you'd get your degree without writing the exams provided you had a reasonable pass record in the exams the previous year. My 1941 standing was OK. I was at the recruiting center faster than you could say Lord Kitchener. But Varsity wasn't going to be hoodwinked by a lot of academic slackers who merely promised to join up in return for a degree. You actually had to be in uniform.

My faithful Saturday afternoons in the Canadian Officer Training Corps (scene: crawling around in High Park, scouring among the bushes and leaves for the enemy; report from the front: couple seen fucking in bushes, shall we surround? instructions back to the front: no, tell the gentleman to withdraw) served no earthly use. The corporal at the Toronto Scottish recruiting desk said they didn't need any officers, thanks, and they weren't signing anybody else at the moment because the lists were full. Same at the navy recruiting depot. The air force was my desperate third choice.

I had to go back twice for the mercury test, palms sweaty. The mercury had nothing to do with radiation. It was a small blob which you were supposed to hold up in a vertical tube by holding your breath for a minute. Purpose? See if you have any guts, the officer said. Despite that, I made it.

I was in Manning Depot in Toronto — with uniform — two days before graduation day. Close. My cousin Herbert had given me a good tip about Manning Depot: shave at night. My beard was light enough so that I wouldn't be detected and punished on early parade for not shaving in the morning. It would mean another fifteen minutes in the sack and no lineups at the wash troughs.

He was right, as he had been about the best way to make axles for our interminable wooden carts and how to find the few trout pools in the creek at the back of the farm in Jacksontown, N.B. Herbert and I had been close friends since 1929 when I took the train alone from Lennoxville, Quebec, to Woodstock, New Brunswick, with a change in the middle of the night at McAdam Junction. I spent every summer on the farm of my mother's brother. It was on the third tier back from the St. John River and on some dewy mornings you could see a coil of fog riding on the river for miles and miles.

They were marvellous summers. We built houses out of potato and fertilizer bags down along the rail fence where we picked, in turn, strawberries, gooseberries, raspberries, and blackberries; we tested our courage by running barefoot across the stubble of a new-mown field, then eased the pain in fresh, warm cowflops. The depression seldom intruded. Once my older cousin John and I took a wagonload of potatoes to the rail siding. It took us all day with the big bay team, Ned and Bob. We got $1.90 for nineteen barrels. My uncle didn't say a word when John gave him the money, but the next day he hauled the rest of his potatoes to the sidehill pasture, dumped them there and ploughed them under.

Herbert joined up long before I did. I saw him once before he was shot down on a bomber run to the Ruhr. His parents waited for months before they found out he had bailed out safely and was in a prisoner-of-war camp. But he didn't survive the camp. A German fighter plane buzzed the camp one day and a wing caught him in the head from behind. A plane at low level gives no warning.

At the end of the war, I went to Jacksontown to see my aunt and uncle and the farm. The long road to the farmhouse comes east down a hill, past the wellhouse and the horsebarn. The farmhouse faces south, so that anybody coming down the road can't be seen from the verandah. I rounded the corner, and my aunt was sitting in her usual bow-back chair, shelling peas in her lap.

She looked up and saw me in my air force uniform. The most wondrous expression of joy came on her face and she threw her arms in the air. She thought it was Herbert, safe as she had prayed despite the terrible telegrams. In a flash, she tried to pretend the greeting was for me. I kissed her on the cheek and she was crying and I have kicked myself in the ass ever since for not giving some warning, a shout, a stone thrown against the barn.

I learned a couple of other things at Manning Depot besides shaving at night. One was to look at the floor before getting out of the bunk.

The bunks in the cow palace, horse palace, pig palace and all the other palaces at the Canadian National Exhibition, the Manning Depot, were two-tiered and close together. I had an old bird over me. The first morning of our cohabitation, I put my bare feet into a pool of vomit. The next morning I swung out on the other side of the bunk and put my bare feet into the same thing. You could never tell whether he was going to puke port or starboard in the middle of the night.

I was still awake one night when he crept in, tanked as usual. I said quite politely, "Why don't you go toss your biscuits in the can before you get into the bunk?"

He paused, then said it didn't sound like a bad idea. He tottered off to the can and came back, he said, much relieved. He kept that routine and I was spared washing my feet before breakfast for the rest of my stay at the Depot. He never woke me once. For an old geezer, he sure was nimble getting into that upper bunk.

Another thing I learned was that stealing is poor policy when it doesn't work. The SPs (special police, though there was nothing special about them) nabbed a corporal one day in the cow palace with more than forty empty wallets in his kitbag. His bunk was near the showers and that's where most wallets were left unattended. The whole crowd of 10,000 of us was marched to the arena for his drumming out of the service. The poor bastard stood in the dirt at the center of the horse ring while his stripes and buttons were ripped off his uniform. They were sliced off so neatly some of us figured it had been done beforehand, leaving them hanging literally by a thread. It was the greatest deterrent to crime I have ever seen. All these years later, I can remember that corporal's name.

Then began months on guard duty at Mimico racetrack. There was nothing to guard, of course. It was a place to put people for a time — part of the human resources pipeline as one would say today. The RCAF had this strange fascination for horses: the CNE, Mimico racetrack, and my next stop was the Hunt Club on Avenue Road, converted into an Initial Training School. There I spun the Link trainer (it may have been the only time this ground trainer had been put into a spin) and flunked out as a pilot. They put me down for navigator and I spent the winter of 1942-43 at Malton airport.

My flight from Malton was my first. As a boy I had watched the barnstormers (there was a landing strip right beside the house of one of my mother's friends at Derby, Vermont) but never had the five dollars to go up, even if I had dared. One Sunday, there was a parachutist and he jumped into Derby Pond when the wind turned on him and everybody ran across the field to see the floating parachute covering his drowned body, like a burial at sea.

Everybody said you always threw up on your first trip, so I did. I sat in the starboard seat beside the pilot, Mr. Quisgaard, and had the round cardboard sick container ready in my hand for miles and miles. Mr. Quisgaard said I'd never throw up again in an aircraft. He was right, though lots of times I wished I had.

I recall vaguely being nervous, nothing like the terror I was to feel later, on squadron. What I liked was the living map below, rivers, lakes and forests, railways and towns. In a plane today, I still stare at the ground like a rube, but I've reached that wonderful age when being taken for a rube doesn't fret me anymore.

Our barracks and classrooms were in overheated H-huts. Our source of recreation was the Trans-Canada Air Lines coffee shop, which had six stools at a dry bar and no tables but a glamorous, big-titted girl who dispensed the coffee. We occupied all the stools but nobody seemed to mind. In that winter, I don't recall seeing a TCA crew, let alone a passenger. With us aloft in Ansons on our night-flying exercises, TCA wisely gave Malton a wide berth.

The twin-engine Anson was a venerable and honorable plane and just the classroom to learn aerial navigation. But there was something about it in winter which the pilots, mostly civilian bush pilots hired specially for this dreary routine, found infuriating. We trainees had to open the hatch above the pilot's head so that we could stick our sextants out to take star shots and more than once I heard above the engines, "Shut that goddam hatch or I'll stuff you through it, along with your goddam sextant."

We plotted the results of our star shots on our maps, as we were supposed to do. They showed us hundreds of miles from where we were supposed to be. But never fear. Those pilots knew those courses we were supposed to be on — Brampton to Chatham, Brampton to Tilbury, Brampton to Owen Sound and Havelock, Brampton to Sharbot Lake. We worked furiously at our cramped tables in the Anson. We would send a written change of course order forward to the pilot. We could see him examine it with raised eyebrows or a shrug but the plane droned on never deviating from the standard route and straight back to base.

On my last night flight to Sharbot Lake, the weather was bad and I kept working as hard as I could to keep from barfing. I passed forward the required instructions on courses and times as we bounced around the sky. To my utter surprise, we landed back at Malton on time. The pilot, Mr. McIssac, turned to me after he had shut down the engines. "Nice navigation, son," he said, keeping a perfectly straight face. Then he winked. I had a total airborne time in training of ninety-seven hours and fifty minutes.

There wasn't much boozing at Air Observer School because you could be on a flight at very short notice. Flying with a hangover in a plane which can't get over the clouds is very debilitating. So there were the langorous evenings watching Big Tits in the TCA coffee shop and listening to Benny Goodman and Peggy Lee on the radio after lights out in the barracks.

Long into the night, I could see from my bunk two red glows across the aisle: the radio dial and the cigarette of one of my classmates. He was still smoking every night when I fell asleep. He was drawn and red-eyed in the morning.

A year later, I learned that when he went out to his plane for his first trip over Germany, he kept throwing up and couldn't get in the plane. They tried to push him into the plane and make him go but he wouldn't. They sent him home and branded him LMF (Lack of Moral Fibre). There but for the Grace of God went all of us.

We were at Y Depot in Halifax, waiting for a boat and in the meantime being tramped on by the pretties at the Saturday night dances. Booze, sweat, and sex, all upright on the dance floor.

Buzz Beurling, the Malta Spitfire ace, was in town on one of those bond drives to which war heroes were regularly subjected. The RCAF paraded Beurling around with pride — as long as he was on the ground. They hated his guts in the air. He was a loner. He had made his mark with the RAF, not with the RCAF, which had rejected him. He wouldn't come to heel and be the tame orderly officer they wanted. They expected him to dress properly and mouth the scripts which public relations officers who had never been in Malta or never flown wrote for him. (A hero friend of mine in early 1945 was pressed into one of these bond tours. He did the Maritimes factory circuit. He spoke only long enough to line up, with hand and eye signals, the best-looking broad in the audience for his evening entertainment. It was his most successful tour since puberty, he said.)

Anyway, Beurling was to give us a pep talk in the station theater. He was preceded on stage by the VD film. This was the movie which warned us — after the Saturday night dance, never before — against syphilis, gonorrhea, and crabs. Near the end, the camera travelled down an enormously long penis (appreciative whistles) and came to a stop at a chancre the size of Vesuvius. The whistles died away. We looked at each other apprehensively, silently vowing never to go for anything worse than the crabs.

Beurling was next. Long nose, that great shock of corn-yellow hair. And those eyes, little milk-blue corneas in huge pupils. Even from the back of the hall, you could see those little flashing pinpoints. No wonder he could shoot like he did. We were transfixed.

He told us a flying story. He was on patrol out of Malta

and got in a dogfight with some Eyeties. I think I can quote him fairly accurately even now: "There was this one plane, all white, absolutely white. And the cockpit sitting up above the fuselage, sitting up there like a great big thumb. I got the pilot in my sights. He tried to turn inside but I just kept following him. I wanted a particular shot. When I fired, I didn't hit the plane itself. I hit the cockpit like I wanted. Blew the cockpit and the pilot's head right off. You should have seen the red blood streaming back over the white fuselage."

Then Beurling threw his head back, yellow hair flying, and laughed — and laughed and laughed. I sat there frozen in my seat, the blood draining out of my face. Jesus, is that what war is like? I hadn't signed up for anything like that.

I saw Beurling in London once in 1944 when I was on ops. I was down from my squadron for the evening (we were only thirty miles away) and trying to get a last drink in the Captain's Cabin near Piccadilly. He was sitting on a bar stool, his back to the bar. As far as I can recall, he didn't smoke and, if he drank at all, it was very little. Anyway, he didn't have a glass. There were five women around him, not bags, gorgeous women. He was laughing and joking, not loudly, not telling war stories, a charmer among a group of good-looking, well-dressed women. Had he been at a party and brought them all with him? Had they deserted their escorts in the bar for those compelling eyes? I never found out. I gazed in wonder and envy, finished my drink and left to catch the last train.

I was attending a Maritimes meeting of The Canadian Press in Sydney in 1948 and took into the meeting the news that Beurling had been killed on takeoff from Rome en route to Israel and his first love, a new war.

Len Tilley, managing editor of the old *Halifax Chronicle*, burst into tears. He kept sobbing for some time. Afterwards I said to him, "You must have known Beurling well."

"I never met him," he said. "It was just that . . . " He looked bewildered and walked away.

One bright March day we were paraded down to the S.S. *Cavina* at Pier 21. A couple of guys tried to slip away and hide when we were in the shed but the SPs were used to that trick and flushed them out. A few of the others hissed at them when they rejoined the ranks but the rest of us didn't say anything. I figured that the guys who did the hissing were more scared than the guys who had made their last stab at AWOL (absent without leave) in Canada.

Nobody cheered us to the pier behind the Nova Scotian Hotel, as those newsreels kept showing. There was no band. Nobody threw up the sash and threw a final kiss. No sobbing women broke away from the crowds on the sidewalk and clutched at marching soldier-boy. Nobody held up a kid to wave goodbye.

We just got on the ship and she sailed, out past the island, the yacht squadron, Point Pleasant Park, and into the open Atlantic. The S.S. *Cavina* was one of the strangest troopships of the war. To begin with, she was an old West Indies banana boat but what was in the hold on that crossing we never found out, except that it wasn't bananas. But the main thing was that the passengers comprised seventy-five women and seventy-five men, all members of the Royal Canadian Air Force, and the bar was open most of the time. The women were about what you'd expect among Canadian WDs (women's division): dumpy, unattractive, big eaters. The men were about the same, though thin, like me. No matter. The trip lasted two weeks and all of us eventually began to look more attractive to one another.

We were somewhere near the middle of the convoy, I suppose, though it was difficult to tell because the ships stretched to the horizon in every direction. We sat out on deck during those cold, windy days, watching the four ships ahead, astern, port, and starboard, until the bar or dining room opened, whichever came first.

There were a few cabins on the top deck with single occupants only. At least, they started out as single occupancy. After a week, they were all double occupancy, all of the time.

When one of the cabineers became exhausted by sex, drink, and food, in that order, he or she simply rented the room to another couple, rates depending on the time occupied.

Usage of the cabins fell off drastically during submarine alarms. Fear knocks hell out of sex drive. I was to find the same thing in London hotel rooms when buzz bombs cut out overhead and started their swift, random-death descent.

Early one morning I was taking a turn about the deck when I noticed that the ship on our starboard side was not the same freighter that had been there the afternoon before. "What happened?" I asked a couple of crew members, who were nearly all limeys.

They just shrugged. "I'm not running the convoy, mate," one said. We could never get any damn information from the crew. In fact, we weren't supposed to talk to them.

The weather got worse and worse. The submarine alarm would go periodically and we'd all get into our greatcoats and lifejackets and go sit in the lounge. We were as quiet as mice, even after just leaving the bar. The next morning, the ships around us would have changed. And there would be gaps in the convoy. But we never saw or heard anything. From late afternoon, the portholes were locked and blacked out. The storm must have drowned the noise of ships blowing up around us, we advised each other. The crew said nothing.

Then one night, about 11 P.M., the submarine alarm bell began ringing continuously. In the four-bunk room where I lived, I put down my poker hand and got into all my heavy clothes. I didn't feel like playing poker anyway because the ship was diving and rocking and yawing. We all trooped into the lounge with our helmets on and sat in the yellow wicker chairs. Then an enormous wave knocked down the door on the top deck and the water cascaded down the stairs into the lounge. "Torpedo!" somebody screamed and we all panicked. If the RCAF had put seventy-five women and seventy-five men on that ship with the expectation that the men would help the women in an emergency, the RCAF had goofed. The women were violently pushed aside as we all rushed to the boat deck, flinging doors open, forgetting the blackout, staggering to the side of the boats, some of us trying to get into them, the crew screaming at us to get back, the ship was OK.

We sat for the rest of the night in the lounge, the water swirling about our ankles. One casualty: one of the men had a broken leg. He was caught in the first rush for one of the doors. He said three women had sandwiched him between them and the door jamb.

The next morning I was walking back and forth on deck, recalling that my jaw had dropped open and that I couldn't close it when that idiot had yelled "torpedo." I was to experience that, and worse, a lot more times.

A member of the crew came up to me with a look of loathing. He stuck his face in mine. "You lousy bastards," he said. "If this ship does catch a packet, we're getting into the boats and leaving every one of you yellow sons of bitches here."

He really said it, and me an air force officer.

We sailed into Liverpool a few days later under a beautiful April sky. We marched off the boat — again, no band — and to a train in the dank station. An old bird was selling sandwiches and I bought one. I bit into it. "What's this?" I asked.

"Watercress. There's a war on, y'know."

CHAPTER TWO

Bournemouth was the bathchair capital of the English seaside. The RCAF took over most of its hotels, some of them well appointed, some of them seedy, to house the people arriving from Canada before they were sent on to operational training units.

I bunked in one hotel (four of us to a room), ate in another, and did guard duty in a third. We paraded every morning in a residential street on the cliff above the seashore. An old gentleman in a bathchair pushed by a middle-aged woman in a bonnet passed us on the sidewalk every morning. He glared at us from under his woollen cap. We had occupied his street, were trampling his grass and probably had shoved him out of the hotel room he had occupied for centuries.

His glares were nothing to those we received in the pub. We unknowingly grabbed the natives' favorite seats when the doors opened. They were lucky to find a place to stand. The pubs were happy new experiences for Canadians used to the dingy taverns of home where one was made to feel uncomfortable, if not immoral.

Some pubs were so crowded in the evening you might wait twenty minutes for a glass, let alone any contents. I got into the habit in some troop-infested towns of carrying a glass or cup in my pocket which I would hand to the barman when I managed to struggle within reach of him. Rumors of quiet, uncrowded pubs spread quickly. You'd whiz out the first opportunity to investigate but they would be the same as all the others, full of troops, the locals struggling gamely to keep a toehold, the Canadians making it impossible for them to do this by tipping the landlord or slipping the barmaids ration coupons left over from leave. For ration coupons, of course, you expected more than a drink.

We farm and village boys became as smooth as silk: "How about one for yourself, Guv'nor?"

The months came and went pleasantly in Bournemouth, a place none of us could have afforded if we'd been paying our own way. The symphony orchestra tottered along with oldsters and we could get in for sixpence. The theater also continued to function. I saw the best Duke Mantee I have ever seen there. An unknown American played the role and never did get famous though he played the part far better than Humphrey Bogart did.

I'm a longtime theater goer. It all stems from my mother taking me to the Lakewood summer stock theater near Skowhegan, Maine, each year we passed through there en route from Stanstead, Quebec, to Jacksontown, New Brunswick, in her 1928 Ford. I remember we had front-row balcony seats one time for *They Knew What They Wanted*. In the scene near the end where the farmer learns his imported bride is pregnant by the hired man, my mother grabbed my sister by the hand and said, "Come, Mary, we have to go to the bathroom." "But I don't want to go to the bathroom," yelled my sister. She was dragged out anyway. I was astonished in later life when she had three children. I guess she found out what pregnant meant after all. I'm not sure I knew myself in Skowhegan, but I was allowed to stay in my seat amid the grumbling customers who could not see or hear, or both, as my sister departed horizontally at the end of my mother's arm.

Sex was not a big subject with my mother. When a neighbor arrived at my uncle's farm with his cow for servicing, my cousins and I took our dress circle seats atop the barnyard fence to watch the delighted bull go into action with his enormously-long, needle-nosed penis. I could hear my mother from the verandah: "David, I need you to turn the washtub." Gawking back over my shoulder, I trudged to the house while my cousins laughed and hooted and hollered.

Where was I?

Bournemouth, being on the south coast, got some of the hit-and-run raids made by the Jerries. One brilliant Sunday afternoon at lunch, when the pubs were crowded, an FW-190 clipped in off the sea and dropped one on the Metropole Hotel. About fifty were killed, mostly Canadian airmen. Killed on active service, as they say.

My friends and acquaintances were posted one by one to operational training units but I couldn't seem to get out of Bournemouth. Finally, I was sent to Cranwell, the site of the Royal Air Force College, for a radio course. Being a college, Cranwell was a stickler for discipline. The group captain halted me on my bicycle one cold day and told me to "take off that simply dreadful turtleneck sweater." My shirt and tie could not be seen. There was one Indian in the officers' mess so we had curried something once a week, which was an improvement on fishpaste and cold toast. (The English invented the toast rack so the toast can cool more quickly.)

You'd think the Brits had never invented or even heard of radar. There we were at Cranwell learning Morse code like railroad telegraphers of long ago. We all got quite good at it, though I never saw a telegraph key after I left the place.

We not only could tap the key but we also learned to repair our radio transmitters and receivers. When a set went U/S (unserviceable), we had a checklist to run down to find the fault. The last check was: "If you cannot see the green light, make sure your helmet isn't down over your eyes."

We darted about over the North Sea off East Anglia, morsing it with some guy on the ground back at Cranwell and hoping to hell we were confusing Jerry into thinking some secret operation was about to unfold.

One day I was standing with Shorty in a bus queue for Lincoln, hoping to make a pub there in time for the opening. The guy next to Shorty, a juicer (Englishman), says: "That's really grisly, isn't it, that WAAF (juicer airwoman) being hacked to death in the shower. I hear they haven't found her head yet."

"For Christ's sake," says Shorty, "I started that rumor two hours ago. And I said she was strangled, not chopped up." Shorty started rumors like that all the time, mostly about parachuting Jerries, in the hope of dispersing queues he was in.

Christmas in the Great Northern Hotel in Lincoln made me yearn for Bowles' Lunch. But there was a war on, y'know. We had a scrawny chicken. Shorty went out to complain about the service and had the waitress in the pantry. Christmas was satisfying for him, anyway.

New orders: Return to Bournemouth. Apart from the locals and the bathchairs, I already held the all-time record for time in Bournemouth. This time I bunked with a pilot who had done twenty-eight days in the glasshouse, the British military prison, spending a lot of his time polishing the soles of his boots. Leave it to the Brits to think up useful things to do. My roommate said plenty of guys were carried away from the place in straitjackets. He wouldn't say what he was in for. I asked him how he had kept his sanity. "I kept my mouth shut, my eyes front, and polished those soles like a son of a bitch," he said.

I watched new arrivals come and go. Even I was getting embarrassed at the length of my idle career. I decided to go see my friend Dave Carr. We had trained together in Canada and he was already on a squadron, 418, then stationed at

Ford, in Sussex. All my squadron time was spent on 418 so I'll give a brief account of its affairs.

To begin with, all RCAF squadrons overseas were numbered in the series 400, and 418 was the 18th squadron authorized by the RCAF. There were also hundreds of Canadians in the Royal Air Force and Douglas Bader's 242 RAF squadron in the Battle of Britain was almost entirely Canadian. By the same token, there were Brits, Yanks, Aussies, and other nationalities on the Canadian squadrons. 418's top ace was an Aussie.

418 was formed in the late fall of 1941 near the village of Debden, in Essex, as part of No. 11 Group, that is, Fighter Command of the RAF. The RCAF had its own group, No. 6, in Bomber Command, but it, too, took orders from the Brits like we did. By the end of the war, and for a long time after it, Canada had the fourth most powerful air force in the world (after the U.S., Britain, and Russia) but took its military orders from the Brits or the Americans — always somebody else. Same with the army. In the First World War, the Canadian Corps was at least kept together as a unit. But in the Second, we allowed part of it to be hived off to Italy, leaving the remainder for Normandy. Everybody commanded us but Canadians. And the navy. We were doing most of the convoy duty in the Atlantic and taking our orders from London. All our nationhood pissed away by chicken governments.

418 in its early days was equipped with the ungainly two-engine Boston, which carried pilot, oberver, and air gunner. Housing was so bad during the first winter that the air and ground crews lived fifty miles apart. Its first operation didn't take place until March 27, 1942, when it bombed, or tried to bomb, an oil refinery in Belgium.

Bombing was not really 418's job, but it carried it on as a sideline — moonlighting, one might say. As the first and only intruder squadron in the RCAF, its main job was to patrol Jerry airfields in Europe at night — especially during bomber raids — and try to pick off night fighters landing or taking off. Other sidelines included train-busting, vehicle-bashing, landing spies, demolition experts and supplies for the French resistance (the Maquis), shooting down the V-1 flying bomb, or doing any nasty little job that came along.

Four aircrews were killed before the squadron went operational. Three more were killed in training before 418 lost its first three-man crew on ops. Twenty-four men dead already for a few bombs dropped, probably harmlessly. Four more crews were lost dropping propaganda leaflets, for God's sake.

In April, 1942, the squadron moved to Bradwell Bay on the forlorn Essex coast. It scored its first kill the following month in a one-in-a-million shot. At night, from 5,000 feet, Al Lukas dropped from his Boston some high-explosive and incendiary bombs on Gilze airfield in Holland. One of them demolished a plane which had just touched down on the runway. Well, you get 'em any way you can. But in exchange for this one score, the squadron had posted eleven crews — thirty-three men — missing.

The squadron's part in the Dieppe raid in August, 1942, was typical of the operation as a whole. Two Bostons were detailed to lay a smokescreen. One turned back because of engine trouble. The other was shot down in the sea by a German Ju-88. The air gunner rescued the pilot and navigator, getting them into a dinghy. All three were picked up by a rescue launch. The pilot died the next day.

The air force, like the army, was fed the same bullshit after the war: Dieppe was a prelude to Normandy and Normandy couldn't have been carried out successfully without the experience of Dieppe. This convenient rationalization was made up after Normandy. At the time of Dieppe there was no suggestion it was a bloody fact-finding mission. The operation was a pure and simple game to relieve the boredom of some underworked British generals. A British waste of Canadian manpower, as the American historian, Samuel Eliot Morison, put it.

In the spring of 1943, the squadron moved to Sussex —

to Ford, near Arundel Castle and the south coast of England — and acquired the twin-engine Mosquito, the plane with which 418 was to make its reputation. RAF squadrons had already had the Mosquito in service for more than a year. This was normal. The RCAF was always last to get new equipment. The RAF even had a photo-reconnaissance version in service before the RCAF obtained the fighter Mossie.

The Mosquito was strictly a war baby — that is, it was designed, tested, built, and put to extensive combat use within the years of the war. It was made of wood — Ecuador balsa, Alaska spruce, Canadian birch and fir, and English ash. That's why they called in furniture makers to help build the plane. In the heat of Burma, some Mosquito wings warped and the glue came unstuck.

The Mosquito carried out nearly every conceivable air combat job. It carried two-ton bombs to Berlin. It shot down enemy planes night or day. It strafed shipping and rail and road traffic. It destroyed German V-1 robot bombs. It broke down the walls of Amiens prison in "Operation Jericho," February 18, 1944, so that French resistance leaders could escape. It demolished Gestapo headquarters in the middle of Copenhagen. It operated as a pathfinder for the heavy bombers, marking targets at night. It photographed the results the next day. With a six-pound anti-tank gun in the nose, it attacked German U-boats.

Generally speaking, its role was murder by night. But it didn't blink at daytime killing.

The Mosquito went through forty-two versions, or marks, including one which could land on an aircraft carrier. The fighter version flown by 418 carried four 20-millimetre cannons and four .303-calibre machine guns, all in the nose. Balls out, it could fly 400 miles an hour but normally cruised at 240. Its range, with extra tanks, was more than 1,700 miles or seven hours. Pilot and navigator sat almost side by side. By "almost" I mean that the navigator's seat was a respectful four inches to the rear of the pilot's.

The Mosquito, or Mossie, or Mozzie, depending on your pronunciation, was originally designed as a fast, unarmed bomber. De Havilland did the design in a moated English manor house, Salisbury Hall, and built the first plane in a makeshift hangar in the cabbage patch behind the house. It was originally known as "Freeman's Folly" because Air Marshal Sir Wilfred Freeman, when chief of Royal Air Force development and production, ordered fifty Mosquitoes against general opposition in the RAF.

The Mosquito was first flown in November, 1940. It flew its first operational sortie only ten months later. The navigator was a peacetime barber named Sowerbutts. The first Canadian-built Mosquito flew at Malton in September, 1942. Malton's de Havilland plant produced 1,134 of the 7,781 Mosquitoes built during the war.

The "Light Night Striking Force" of Mosquitoes raided Berlin 170 times, thirty-six of these on consecutive nights. The Mossie could carry as big a bomb load to Berlin as the U.S. Flying Fortress, which needed an eleven-man crew. The Mosquito flew so often to Berlin that its raids were known as the Berlin Express and the routes taken as platforms one, two, and three.

Six Canadian squadrons flew the Mosquito overseas: 400 squadron used it for photo-reconnaissance; 404 as a rocket-firing coastal fighter; 406, 409, and 410 as a night fighter; and 418 as a night intruder. 418 became the highest-scoring squadron in RCAF history: 105 planes destroyed in the air, seventy-three on the ground, nine probables, 103 damaged, and eighty-three V-1s destroyed.

The Mosquito wasn't always the wooden wonder, the description awarded it by the public relations men. Just a day or two after I joined 418, a Mosquito was flying straight and level over the airfield in daylight when the fabric on the starboard wing shredded and the plywood peeled back like wet bark on a cedar. The pilot and navigator had no time to get out and died as their one-wing Mosquito ploughed into the ground a few miles away and exploded.

After a year and a half of operations, 418 had destroyed only seven enemy aircraft. With the Mosquito, the squadron doubled that score in less than a month. But there were still far more squadron dead than German casualties — forty crews.

In February of 1944, alone, the squadron destroyed twenty-four planes in the air and on the ground. The reason for this success was the partial switch to daylight operations, which were far more dangerous but paid off handsomely. A double kill for a crew on a single sortie was common.

It was at about this time that I went to Ford to spend a couple of days with Dave Carr. He introduced most of the members of the squadron to me in the mess and at the Arundel Arms, a pub better known as the "Shaky Do." A rough translation of "shaky do" is "a very frightening affair" or "Jesus, was my ring twitching." I memorized as many names and faces as I could, then went to RCAF headquarters in London and obtained an interview with a flight lieutenant in personnel. I said I wanted to be posted to 418 squadron rather than serve another sentence in Bathchair City.

"Why 418?" he asked.

"All my friends are there," I said and rattled off all the names of all the guys Dave had introduced at Ford, being careful to skip the officer commanding on the grounds that my social position would hardly qualify me to list him as a friend. In a few days, I was posted to the Mosquito Operational Training Unit (OTU) at High Ercall in Shropshire.

High Ercall — we called it High Fuckall — rested on a wide plateau which sloped away gently on all sides. The slope was as deceiving as that of Parliament Hill in Ottawa. I'm out of wind when I reach the front entrance under the Peace Tower, just as I was pooped pedalling my bicycle from our moth-eaten barracks off the airfield to the base at High Ercall.

I have two memories of High Ercall. One is the stab of a

flashlight out of a barracks window into the neighbouring field to pinpoint a fellow trainee having it off with a sheep. The other has to do with flying.

First, it was back to the old Anson to learn how to work the Gee box. Gee transmitters around the British Isles pumped out signals which you could read in green blips on the black face of the box and which were represented as lines on a map you had with you. You tuned in two Gee stations on the box in the plane and took a reading of your position along each line. Where the two lines crossed on your map, presto, that's where you were. Gee wasn't of much advantage to 418 because we operated at too low a level for it to lead us across the enemy coast at precisely our chosen spot. But it was helpful when we were nearing the English coast on the way home.

The Gee instructors scared the hell out of us by warning us in the Anson: "Watch the blackout. Keep those lights off." Why were they so jumpy? I wondered at the time. Just nervous, burned-out navigators, I figured. It wasn't long before I found out that, compared with me, they were as nervous as the Rock of Gibraltar.

An Anson pilot informed me that more than one Anson trainer had been shot down by German intruders and that the Gee instructors were more worried about their navigational reputations than anything else: it would be just plain laughable for an intruder instructor to be shot down by an intruder.

After the Anson, we tried the Gee box in the Mosquito. And the rest of the time was spent map-reading in daylight. Bump-bump-bump around the damn English countryside at low level, and by low level I mean pulling up to go over the trees.

The Canadian navigators flew with the English instructor pilots at the start of training. There were Canadian trainee pilots around the station and we saw them in the mess, but there was little or no contact at first. Then we were thrown together in a classroom for a lecture and after that we began to have a few drinks together. But there wasn't much camaraderie between the Canadian pilots and navigators, even though we were surrounded by Englishmen (in the local pub, we couldn't even understand the dialect of the farmers).

The last Englishman I ever flew with was Flight Sergeant Hintchliffe. We went up map-reading for an hour and fifteen minutes one April morning. I remember him because he was dead the next day. In the Mosquito, the switches for the main fuel tanks were between the buttocks of pilot and navigator. Usually the navigator handled the fuel cocks but the pilot could also reach the switches, though he couldn't see them. Hintchliffe was coming in for a perfectly normal landing when suddenly the engines quit and he dived straight into the deck with his student navigator. Oddly, there was no fire. When they got the broken bodies out, they found that the student's parachute harness had somehow got twined around the fuel cocks and when he had leaned forward he had turned the switches to "off." There was no time for Hintchliffe to recover. A freak accident. The trouble is, the freak ones kill you just as dead as the straightforward, reasonable ones.

We religiously read the green notice board in the mess. It was crammed with instructions. Do. Don't. Mostly don't. The board was attached to the brick wall of the narrow passage between the dining room and the bar.

One day I found my name was on the crew board beside that of Flying Officer S.P. Seid, pilot. Nobody had asked whether I wanted to fly with him. I got the dreadful feeling that I was a navigational leftover, the last navigator to be picked for crewing with a pilot, the one left standing when the piano stopped for musical chairs. All this was soon confirmed.

I went into the tiny bar. It was crowded. The old hands, the instructors, were drinking out of their own pewter mugs, the newcomers from glasses that the girl behind the bar washed by dipping them for a second into the sink of cold water under the counter.

A pilot approached me. He was tall, though not quite as tall as I — however, he was dark and handsome. His upper lip had a peculiar little curl, as if he could switch a smile into a sneer in a flash, or the other way round. There were a lot of black hairs on the backs of his big hands.

"You McIntosh?"

"Yes."

"I'm Seid. What are you drinking?"

"Brown ale." Seid went to the bar and came back eventually with a bitter.

"No brown ale," he said. "I don't know how you drink that piss. I drink scotch. When they haven't got scotch, I don't drink anything."

Well, that was a good feature, I thought. During the war in England, scotch, if there was any, always ran out in about five minutes. No drunken pilot for me. There were no seats so we stood against the brick wall.

Seid was blunt if nothing else: "Everybody else is crewed up. You're the last navigator available."

"And you're the last pilot," I said. This was dangerous talk on my part. You didn't take cracks at a guy when your life literally depended on his flying ability. He smiled and the smile didn't turn into a sneer.

I pressed my advantage. "Why are you the last pilot?"

"I'm dangerous. I talk back to instructors and senior officers. And I flew under the Jacques Cartier Bridge."

Christ. A daredevil. A sober daredevil. (I checked later and he really had flown a Harvard trainer under the Jacques Cartier Bridge. But a lot of other guys had, I was told reassuringly.)

"Why are you the last navigator?"

"I've been around in England for a year without doing anything except go to radio school. But I had good marks at AOC (air observer school) in Malton."

This time he did sneer, slightly. "Some recommendation. Can you navigate a Mosquito?"

"I think so. You can ask Flight Lieutenant Green over

there. He took me on a low level when I had a gin hangover and I found all the pinpoints, including the ruins of some abbey off in some trees somewhere."

"Are you hung over all the time?"

"No. I wasn't supposed to fly that day but Green said the weather was good, he felt like flying, and I had to go."

Seid went over to Green and I watched them talking for a couple of minutes. He came back. "He says you were pretty good. What about night?"

A reasonable question, inasmuch as most of 418's work was at night. "A total of two hours and fifty minutes," I said.

"Jesus," Seid said.

"That's not counting my Anson night time in Malton, twenty-seven and a half hours."

"Jesus," he repeated. I went to get another beer and to see if there was any scotch (there wasn't).

"Look," he said, when I got back to the brick wall, "I've waited a long time to get to a squadron. I'm so goddam good I got stuck as an instructor for over a year and I don't want to hang around at any goddam OTU." He meant that he didn't want any navigator who might screw things up and get washed out of the course, leaving him to crew up again while all his mates went off to squadron.

"We don't seem to have any choice," I said. He shrugged in agreement. He often shrugged like that, I was to find.

We finally got around to the inevitable question: Where you from?

He was from San Francisco. His first name was Sidney because his father had been born in Sydney, Australia, but thought the Australians spelled it Sidney. He had come to Canada and joined the RCAF before Pearl Harbor, that is, before the Americans were officially into the war. He could have switched to the United States Air Force and doubled his pay but he hadn't — and didn't. He was twenty-three and single.

But he had a worrisome piece of news for me. He was a Jew (that part didn't bother me) and felt pretty strongly that he would like to kill as many Germans as possible (that part did). That's all I needed, a guy who wanted to win the Victoria Cross and who didn't care all that much whether it was posthumously. Why didn't he fly Spitfires or anything else which didn't require a navigator?

Well, maybe it was all talk-talk, like so much of pilot self-advertisement we heard all the time. Then again, it might not be. Christ, a Jewish Billy Bishop with an unwilling occupant of the starboard seat.

We ran through the rest of the routine: When ya get into the air force? Where ya train? How long ya been over here? The main purpose of these exchanges was to let the other man know you (a) had been in the air force longer ("Get some time in, chum") or, (b) at least had been overseas longer. Having discovered that you hadn't been either usually ended a conversation — and men with operational time seldom spoke to men in training. You stayed in your own crowd (same length of service, same time overseas) and hoped to get in enough time or operations to be able to shit on those with less time and fewer ops.

We flew together the very next day for the first time. We were up only ten minutes. The port wing tank fell off on takeoff and Seid did a quick circuit and landed. I liked the way that big hairy right hand gripped the stick and how the big hairy left hand gripped the throttles.

"Did you like my navigation?" I asked. I regretted that.

The very next night, we went up for two and a half hours of map-reading. Piece of cake. We were all over hell's half acre and arrived back at our field — or a field, as it turned out. The station was flashing K-dash dot dash. High Ercall was flashing Y-dash dot dash dash. Hell, I thought, I wonder why High Ercall dropped that last dash. Anyway, we were in the circuit and the intercom was loud and clear.

We landed at Ashbourne, eight miles from High Ercall. What had happened was that the two stations were so close together the High Ercall controller on the ground thought we were in the High Ercall circuit and we naturally thought so too.

Well, no damage done, or not much. A quick turn-around and off to High Ercall. "Sorry, chaps," said the bastard limey controller. "We're closed down for the night. You can bunk here and take off in the morning."

It was doubly embarrassing in the morning. Ashbourne was home for a bunch of ancient troop transport planes. The Mosquito stood out among these uglies like a rose among bloodroot. Every damn pilot in the mess asked what kind of trouble we had run into.

"Navigational trouble," Sid barked. The RAF lads had a jolly laugh all round.

Goodbye High Fuckall, hello Bournemouth, I thought. But, back at base, nobody said anything, and matters improved for me next day when Sid boiled over the radiators as we were sitting on the tarmac. I was smart enough to keep my mouth shut.

Things went along routinely after that until we made a simulated night intruder run to Long Kesh in Northern Ireland. The idea was that the Irish Sea would act the substitute for the North Sea and English Channel until we got to the real thing. We groped our way to Long Kesh and back OK. But when we were in the circuit preparing to land — at High Ercall this time — the undercarriage wouldn't go down. At least the light which was supposed to show that it was locked down didn't come on. I had always been a bit jumpy in the air. This time I was really frightened.

With throttles pulled back, Sid flew low past the control tower. "The undercarriage seems OK," the controller said. It was in the "down" position. Whether it was locked was something else.

Sid was calm. "Push down that button at your left heel," he said. It was part of the emergency hydraulic system. It wouldn't go down.

"Push harder." I put my left heel on it and stamped as hard as I could. Nothing happened.

"Start pumping," Sid ordered.

"What?"

He pulled out a metal bar and showed me where to attach it to the emergency hydraulics on the floor. "Pump up and down."

I pumped like a madman. I undid the straps which fastened me into the seat so that I could lean farther forward and use longer strokes. The light didn't come on and I was sweating. Sid flew by the control tower again.

"It looks OK," the controller repeated. "But land on the grass beside the runway in case it isn't." We went around again.

"You shut off the gas when I tell you," Sid said.

"Shut off the gas?" I squeaked.

"It helps if you don't want to feed a fire."

"Fire?"

We went around again. I was still pumping furiously. We came into the funnel on final approach.

Sid looked across at me. "You'd better do your straps up." Jesus, I was sitting there as free and easy as if I were in a buggy seat. I scrambled, all thumbs, to refasten the straps.

"Keep pumping," Sid said. My arm was just a blur, it was pumping so fast.

"Now," Sid barked. We were a couple of feet off the deck, above the grass beside the runway. The airfield lights were on despite the blackout.

"Now?"

"The gas, goddam it."

I twisted the fuel cocks and the plane went silent, like a leaf falling in still air. We floated. I couldn't feel any wheels touch down. Then the props hit and pretzelled into funny shapes, like Dali paintings. The engine cowlings slid along the grass. Sid stayed right on line parallel with the runway. There was grinding, rending, and crunching; sparks flew all over the place. My shoulders ached where the straps had dug in.

"You can stop pumping," Sid said. I was still at it. And then he shouted, "And get the Christ out!"

I punched the strap fastener to free myself. The tiny door was by my right foot. I got it open and crawled out. I didn't need Sid's shove in the ass. He was a tenth of an inch behind me. We ran like the wind. But there was no fire, no explosion. The Mosquito lay there, crumpled. Its back was broken, just behind the cockpit.

The engineering officer, white-haired, a white moustache, called on us the next morning. We got into his jeep and rode to where they'd pulled the wreck just off the perimeter track. The engineering officer crawled in the door, put his finger on the button I had been trying to push down and pushed it down easily.

"Must have come unjammed in the crash," I said.

"Did you lift up the safety catch underneath?" the engineering officer asked. "It's there so you don't accidentally push down that button with your foot."

I was standing beside the door with Sid. The engineering officer, inside, couldn't see our faces. "Certainly," I said.

Sid looked at me and he knew and I knew he knew and he knew that I knew he knew. My left arm was twitching, as if I were still pumping that lever.

Later, in the mess, Sid said: "It's lucky for you that I boiled over those rads. It's now two mistakes for you and one for me. We're going to get through this course if it kills us."

We did a final intruder to Limivaddy in Northern Ireland on June 4 and set out by train for 418 squadron on the south coast of England. I had a total flying time since joining the air force of 127 and one-half hours day, forty-four hours night. I was ready (the manuals said) for ops.

I knew there was something screwy when we got to London after the usual execrable train ride in the usual jammed and fetid compartment. We went into a bar and Sid had three scotches in a row.

"Where in hell is everybody?" I asked. We didn't know but everybody was landing in Normandy. It was D-Day. We were probably the only two warriors in all of London. It was damned embarrassing. When we left the bar in the Regent

Palace and hailed a cab for Waterloo, people were staring at us as if we wearing white feathers.

"Well, everybody can't be at the front the first day," I said to Sid defensively.

"Yeah, but we don't have to be out in broad daylight like this."

We caught a train for a destination familiar to me — Bournemouth — but we got off at Christchurch, a few miles before Bournemouth, and a place where I had already tried (and failed) to find that wartime treasure — an uncrowded pub. There were army convoys all over the place, emptying southern England of soldiers where they had been holed up for as much as four and a half years.

We telephoned our station, Holmsley South, and a truck appeared after a while. We stowed our kitbags and haversacks and gas masks in the back of the truck and got in with the driver. "Bloody convoys," he said.

We always travelled light. In the haversack shaving gear, dry socks, a shirt, some underwear, Brasso, brush and button stick (for cleaning buttons without getting the Brasso on the tunic) and, always, something to read to combat the eternal boredom. Everything else went in the kitbag, including greatcoat for winter, spare uniform, if any, and, on top, my books. The trouble was I had to ditch my books as I went along because the kitbag wouldn't allow me to keep older purchases. I had to discard all my Simenons, for instance. Once I reached the squadron I didn't do any book reading. Apprehension about the next trip destroyed concentration at all times of day and night. I don't recall that any of the fliers ever read anything apart from stories about themselves in the London papers. (My colleagues made the front pages fairly often in the days before and after D-Day. Their operations were daring — foolhardy would be my word — and they were taking the war, or a little bit of it, to the Jerries.) Anyway, the kitbag didn't hold many books but it was a corker: it never got lost; it never fell open; it was never holed. I continued to use it in peacetime moving about Canada.

418 had moved to Holmsley South from Ford, I guess to make room for the day fighters. It was near the edge of the New Forest and the mess was a girls' school nestled among some trees. Sid and I moved into the top floor of a two-storey barracks. The next day, Sid's good friend, Ben, another American, and his navigator took the room next door to us.

With my gear put away, I went to the mess to look for Dave Carr. He was missing. He and his pilot had been on their twenty-third sortie, a trip over Denmark, got shot up, ditched in the sea, got out, made it to shore and were put in a prisoner-of-war camp for the duration. Word had come back fairly quickly on what had happened and that they were safe, or as safe as anybody could be in a German POW camp. After the war, Dave told me the first thing he learned in the prison: "Don't bend over in the shower to pick up the soap. Push it with your foot, get your back to the wall, then pick it up, but even then be damn quick about it."

With Dave gone, I had no coach, so to speak. Sid and I were on our own like every other rookie team. It was said that if you made it through the first seven trips you had enough experience to give you a pretty good chance of surviving a whole tour, which was at least thirty trips and usually thirty-five on 418 but often more because some of the trips were pretty short. All a short trip meant to me was that I was scared for a shorter period of time than on a long trip.

CHAPTER THREE

Sid and I reported the next morning to flight operations in a large building beside the field. The furnishings were sparse, as they always were in a flight building: a board listing crews and their assignments, maps on the walls, a couple of telephones, some chairs, and a large table for the navigators to work out their flight plans. The real work was done by the ground crew in the hangars on the far side of the field.

On the first day, Sid and I did a familiarization flight of the area, just so that we would know where Holmsley South was in relation to towns, seacoast, railways, villages, roads and so forth around and about. We also did a cross-country, low-level navigation trip to Ford and back and that night went out to play around with searchlights. We were training and the searchlight crews were training — neither of us was any hell. They couldn't find us very often but when they did con us, we couldn't evade as well as we should have.

On the second day, we did a midnight cross-country and, on the third afternoon when we went down to the flight to look at the crew board, we were down for a real operation that night.

"Christ, that's not much training," I said, my bowels flipping over.

"You're as ready as you'll ever be," Sid said.

"Christ," I repeated, "we've only flown six hours since we got here."

"Keep your voice down," Sid said. "Do you want everybody here to know you're scared shitless?" He always hit the nail on the head like that. I looked around the room. There were some real hot-shot fliers on this squadron and I didn't like it at all.

Bob Kipp and Pete Huletsky, his navigator, eleven destroyed.

Stan Cotterill and Pop McKenna, four destroyed on one night trip.

Don MacFadyen and Pinky Wright, six destroyed.

My pilot was keen enough without these examples but there were worse.

Charlie Scherf, the squadron's top ace, had just left the squadron with a record of twenty-three destroyed, five of them on one operation. To my mind, Scherf was deranged. He had finished his tour and been sent to Intruder Control in London. But he'd take a forty-eight-hour leave to visit 418. Instead of sitting around and chewing the fat and feeling wonderful not flying, he'd team up with somebody and off they'd go on a daylight operation to the south of France or the Baltic or Czechoslovakia or somewhere and shoot down some more planes. He'd added seventeen to his score while on leave, for God's sake.

"What a shooter," Sid said.

"Yeah, yeah," I said.

And what an example that crazy Merv Sims had set. He shouldn't even have been flying. He had been on the squadron in 1942 when his Boston crashed into Mount Snowden in Wales. Merv was the only survivor — barely. He was found after lying in the wreck for three days. He had a broken back, a fractured skull, brain concussion, broken leg, broken thumb, and gangrene had set in in some of his injuries. He was in hospital seven and a half months. Not only was he back flying with 418, he had destroyed six Jerries.

Why didn't guys like that just go home and stop setting these outlandish targets for impressionable young pilots to shoot at?

During the time I was on the squadron, there were at least ten aces (we never used that word ourselves) — that is, crews which had destroyed at least five German planes. The squadron was doing so well militarily, that it even received a visit from Air Marshal Breadner, the boss of the RCAF overseas who didn't command anything (the Brits did) except the paper administration. The squadron then had destroyed more than 100 Jerries and its keenness, as our PR man said, knew no bounds. Mine had plenty of bounds.

Churchill had shown up briefly during an inspection of D-Day preparations. The squadron was adopted by the City of Edmonton, which meant a good supply of cigarettes and food parcels. And then the King had come down to hand out medals: a gong parade, it was called. When I arrived on 418 it seemed to me that every flier on the squadron was wearing a Distinguished Flying Cross for some ridiculous show of bravery which could kill one, and often did.

This squadron, in short, was going to be a very difficult place to mask cowardice. Even before my first trip, it was tough enough.

"Where are we going?" Sid asked.

"Morlaix and Lannion," I said, reading it off the crew board, chalked in neatly after our number, with the scheduled time off, 2330 hours.

"Where in hell are they?" Sid asked.

"I haven't a clue," I said. We looked at the big map on the wall and concentrated on northern France. We were on a "nursery op," as first trips were called, and wouldn't be expected to go very far over enemy territory. With some relief, I spotted Morlaix and Lannion. They were only a few miles inside the Brittany coast. A fast getaway if any trouble, I thought immediately.

Sid was burned up. "You call that a trip?" he said. He looked back at the board and noted that Russ Bannock, also fresh from Canada, had been assigned a field down near Paris for patrol. Bannock was one of those fliers — MacFadyen was another — who had been stuck in Canada for years as a flying instructor and then as an instructor of the instructors. They could fly rings around most pilots, but up to now had never been on ops. It didn't take Bannock long to show how good he was: he knocked down a Jerry on his very first trip. He caught an Me-110 on the runway at Avord and killed it on one run.

Sid was not envious. He was just competitive. "Let's get our NFT done," Sid said.

NFT was night flying test. Before every operation, you checked your aircraft. This meant, in effect, you flew every afternoon you were on night duty. The main purpose was to check the engines and all the equipment to see that everything was working smoothly. The navigator went along for the ride and had a choice of staring at the instruments or the ground. I always took the opportunity of checking the general lay of the land. I abhorred the thought of ever again landing at the wrong field unnecessarily. I had only one thrill on an NFT and it wasn't with Sid. It was after I had been on the squadron a few months. Stu Woolley's navigator was sick, hung over, shacked up in London or something and Stu asked me to perform the NFT honors with him. I thought it would give me a chance to compare squadron pilots. The comparison was all in Sid's favor. Stu got fooling around, we were in cloud and the first thing I knew the cartridges for the Very pistol were dancing in front of my eyes as they floated around the cockpit. We were in a goddam spin. We came out of cloud way over on our side but we had enough altitude, thank God, for Stu to get lined up on the real horizon and get us straightened out. I didn't have time, really, to figure out what had happened. Stu tried to pass it off as an air pocket but I could see the knuckles on his hand around the stick were as bloodless as I knew my face was.

"No need to mention that to anybody," Stu said lightly.

"OK," I said, and I never mentioned it to Sid or anybody else to this moment. Stu was killed in a night crash in a CF-100 jet after the war at St. Hubert. Kipp was killed there too, after the war, about the same time Scherf was killed back home in Australia at a level crossing.

The NFT provided about the only occasion when we could talk to the ground crew, apart from the pub. At the night takeoff there was no time for talk and when we got back we didn't feel like it or were too pooped.

The ground crew had worked all morning tuning up our plane. They expected us to do the NFT about 3 P.M. so they could fix any faults Sid might find. They were out again at night for takeoff, and there when we got home, sometimes not much before dawn.

Generally, we flew the same plane, but when it went in for a major engine change or something like that, we took another. We took the truck from the ops room down to dispersal and walked out to the Mosquito M for Mother. "How is it, Hal?" Sid asked.

We hadn't done an operation yet but Sid had already taken the trouble to learn the names of the ground crew. He was speaking to the rigger, a farmer from Saskatchewan. "She should be OK," Hal said.

We talked about the weather and a pub in Christchurch. Although we hardly knew the ground crew, we both sensed how important they were to us. As it turned out, we never had engine trouble when our own crew was on duty. When it was another crew, things were different.

We climbed up the ladder and did the test. We were back in fifteen minutes. "Fine, just fine," Sid told the crew. "Purred like two kittens."

We went to the mess for high tea, the usual toast and fishpaste served in glass jars so small it was impossible to get the knife past the neck. I suppose that was the object. I didn't feel like eating. All I was thinking about was the Morlaix-Lannion trip. All this damn training and waiting and boredom and here I was going to some godforsaken airfield in Brittany from which, probably, no plane of any nationality had ever flown. Well, better that than Berlin for Op. No. 1.

We fiddled around till dusk. I pretended to read a newspaper. When we got to the ops room, I got out my maps and started work on a flight plan. I had been given, on arrival at the squadron, about twenty maps of the Continent and Britain. Mickey Cochrane, a navigator who was starting his second tour on the squadron, showed me how to trim and fold them so they took up the least space and could be extended as a trip progressed across Europe and — I hoped — back again.

I spread out southern England, our standard map because Holmsley South was on it, and northern France. Then I drew a heavy pencil line from Holmsley to Morlaix. I measured the course in degrees and distance. We cruised at 240 miles an hour, or four miles a minute. So I divided the distance by the speed and got the time. That's all there was to it. I filled out the appropriate numbers on a sheet provided: course, distance, and time.

All those months learning and practising navigation by the stars, then learning to talk-talk by Morse. All for nothing. We flew so low that we discounted the winds. So I didn't even have to work out a course which allowed for wind, the purported essence of aerial navigation. And I was never allowed to talk with the control tower. That was Sid's prerogative.

In practice, our navigation on 418 squadron boiled down to this: we took a long pencil and marked it off in inches. Each inch was four miles or one minute. The pencil laid between two points on the map gave us the rough course and the notches in it gave us the time and distance. We had only three basic tools: the pencil, the map, and the flashlight to see the map. That was in the air. On the ground, you worked out as much basic information as you could use with proper compass and ruler. But as soon as your pilot went haring off after an enemy plane or a train or a convoy, all that prepared stuff was out and you were left with the three original basics. To think of the nights I had frozen my fingers sticking that sextant out of the hatch of an Anson to get those beautiful, if wildly inaccurate, star shots. The pencil is mightier than the sextant in my navigation system.

Sid never bothered me about the routes I picked though later on, when we were doing daylight trips into Europe, it was important that we study the maps together to make sure we knew all the landmarks (pinpoints) we would have to rely on to get us to target and back. He left me to the plotting while he chewed the fat with the other pilots, mostly about the weather and tactics and the price of broads in the bar of the Regent Palace.

After I finished my navigation preparations, I sat down in one of the chairs along one wall of the ops room. This was waiting time, waiting for 2330 takeoff, waiting for varied and frightening imaginings. I tried to talk to Doug, who was also making his first trip, but I couldn't really think of anything to say I was so preoccupied with my fears. Doug's pilot, Ben, Sid's friend, was yakking it up with Sid as if the two had done four tours. They had been friends since flying instructor days. Ben was careful and precise.

At last it was time to go. But it was all a last-minute scramble, as if I'd been given thirty seconds warning of the trip. I had flying boots but forgot to put them on. It was June and we didn't fly high where it was cold. I wore plain, ordinary service shoes and battledress, which was tunic and pants. I did remember to put on the parachute harness and the Mae West, the bulky life preserver with its little red lights so we could be spotted floating in the dark sea. I took my parachute, dinghy, helmet, and a canvas bag containing maps, log, pencils, two spare flashlights (there was one flashlight in the aircraft) and plastic compass.

We left the ops room — Sid, Ben, Doug and I — without any ceremony. Nobody said anything. The flight commander didn't wish us good luck or offer any advice. The intelligence officer didn't even look up from his dirty book. He read only books about flagellation, and the *London Daily Mirror*. We just went outside into the dark and got in the truck and were driven out to the aircraft. Sid and Ben sat with the driver, Doug and I were on the hard bench in the back. Pilots always went first, navigators drawing up the rear like spear carriers or food tasters. Crews were usually known by the pilot's name alone. If the navigator was mentioned, he was tacked on, like a wife's name.

The four of us got out of the truck, and Sid and I walked toward M for Mother, parked outside its sandbagged bay. "See ya boy," Sid said to Ben. We walked down the taxi strip, beside the amber lights, and we could hear the hard boots of the ground crew as the men scurried about, running the battery cart into position, wiping off the windscreen. Hal was standing under the starboard wing, holding the ladder that took us up through the tiny side door into our office.

"Bit cool, isn't it?" said Hal. I noticed for the first time that it was.

"Everything OK?" Sid asked.

"Fine," Hal said.

Sid threw his chute and dinghy through the door and climbed up. He sat in my seat while he stored the chute in his own cramped space behind the stick. I stood beside Hal, looking at the clouds drifting across the face of the moon behind the thin pine trees at the far side of the field. All of a sudden, I remembered I had forgotten to have a leak. Discreetly, I ducked under the Mosquito's belly and took up a position under the port wing. I peed.

Sid was yelling something from inside. I finished and went back to the ladder. "Don't you want to come?" Sid asked.

I went up one step on the ladder and handed my maps to Sid. Then I put my chute on the floor and tossed the dinghy into my seat. I climbed up the other two steps and struggled through the door. My Mae West caught on the hinge and I couldn't free it right away.

"You coming or not?"

"I'll be there in time for takeoff," I said.

I ripped the Mae West only slightly getting clear of the door. I plunked myself down on the dinghy, the little rubber lifeboat all done up in a neat square package. The rubber sucked out your piles if fear didn't. I felt for the hooks on my harness and snapped the dinghy clamps into them. If I jumped, the dinghy came with me. If I didn't, I unhooked it at the end of the trip.

"Can you help with these damn straps?" Sid asked.

I reached over and found Sid's straps, which locked him in his seat, and passed them over his shoulders. Two went over his shoulders, two came up from the sides of the seat. Sid gathered the four together and locked them together with the brass pin. I did the same, twisting in the narrow seat. My parachute was on the floor between my feet. There we were, as snug as two peas in a pod. This was no place for claustrophobia. I had room enough to twirl a pencil between my fingers and that was about it.

I felt in the small, upended box at my right knee to make sure all the maps were in place. First the map of southern England, then the Gee grid chart of the English Channel, then France, Belgium, and Holland, western Germany and southern Germany, central Germany and eastern Germany and so on, just in case.

Hal took the ladder away and then came close, his chin just below the edge of the doorway. "OK, Sid?"

"OK." The door slammed shut and Hal turned the latch from the outside.

Sid had already adjusted his helmet and plugged in his intercom. He pulled open the small panel of perspex near his left cheek and yelled through the opening, "Contact!"

Near the tail the man at the battery cart echoed: "Contact!" There was a whirring sound when Sid pressed hard on the button in the instrument panel in front of him for the port engine. The prop chugged over slowly once or twice, missed fire, then burst into a roar which cut off all other sound.

A second later Sid pressed the button for the starboard engine. Blue flames vomited from the exhaust. Then the flame dampers came into play. An open exhaust was as secret as a searchlight playing on you. Sid pulled back on the throttles until both engines were at taxiing speed. I got my helmet on and plugged in in time to hear Sid say, "What's the first course, boy? I'll stick her on here now."

I had to scramble about a bit, fishing the flashlight out, finding the flight plan, double-checking where the miniscule ray of light fell on the lines of courses and times. "One-nine-two. One-ninety-two. One-niner-two."

Sid put the course on the compass ring. "Check the lights?"

"I will."

"Gas?"

"I will." I put the flashlight and flight plan down on the narrow space of seat at my left side and felt to see that my pencils were securely in place in my inside pocket. Then I took the aircraft flashlight, another tiny light at the end of a long cord, and peered at the gas gauges. Full. Then I checked the lights. Only the belly light was on to show our presence to other planes on the ground. The theory was that we were invisible from the air with only a belly light showing.

"All OK, Sid," I said.

"Don't forget that belly light after we get off the ground."

I suppose I should have resented the constant repetition of such instructions, which had been going on since training unit. Sid knew that I checked every time and I knew that Sid knew that I did. But it was a small piece of insurance in an uninsurable world.

"Credo two-nine. OK to taxi?" Credo was the squadron call sign. Two-nine was our individual call sign.

"OK two-nine." Control tower wasn't verbose. The chocks were pulled away from the wheels and out in front of us Hal was signalling with two waving flashlights to pull out onto the taxi strip.

The Mosquito moved ahead slowly and wind gushed out behind us. With a frantic motion Hal circled his right arm and Sid ran up the port engine, pulling us around onto the perimeter track leading to runway two-seven. We slid by the blue and amber lights on either side marking the taxi strip. The lights stopped just at the head of the runway. Clamping his black-haired hand over the throttles at his left side, Sid ground them forward notch by notch, first one, then the other. The needles marking the revolutions per minute raced around their dials and the Mosquito shuddered as they reached 3,000. My stomach rocked. Sid eased back the throttles and switched on the tower.

"Credo two-nine. OK for takeoff?"

"Credo two-niner. OK." More loquaciousness. You'd think control could say good luck or goodbye, happy motoring or something.

Sid turned the plane onto the runway into the flarepath. I was always fascinated, by exultation or horror, I was never clear which, by those two strings of lights stretching away into my future.

"All OK, boy?"

"OK, boy." I always had a little difficulty getting it out. I was never ready, of course.

Sid pushed forward on the throttles again, this time with brakes off. The eleven tons of wood, steel, gas, and us lurched ahead. The speed increased; the tail came up. The speed rose some more. We were going now. I looked out my side at the control tower as we flashed by. In the dimmed-out, bluish interior I could see indistinct figures standing stock-still.

My right hand went to the row of switches at my right side and carefully selected the one to switch off the belly light. My left hand felt for the fuel cocks as I made sure, for the tenth time, that they were pushed all the way down to the "on" position. Near the end of the flarepath, Sid pulled the stick toward him. M for Mother freed herself from the macadam, lifted, whisked at 100 miles an hour past the end, over the unseen trees. Sid reached forward and yanked up on the undercarriage lever. Seconds later, the lever dropped. The wheels were fully up.

I got my pad out, produced a pencil, got the flashlight, looked at my watch and wrote: AB (for airborne) 2330.

"Belly light off?" asked Sid. How much goddam insurance does he need, I thought. But I didn't say anything. You don't make flip remarks to a guy who can push throttles and put a plane into the air.

Sid held her steady. The altimeter turned slowly, as slowly as the second hand on your watch. You didn't turn or climb too fast in a Mosquito until you had height and speed. Even at cruising speed, you didn't fool around very much. The Mosquito was meant for straight and level flying. So was I. We were a perfect match. Of course you had to crank her around some in difficult spots, but you didn't deliberately try to roll her or do falling-leaf stunts.

Sid brought M for Mother around slowly, back over the field. This was for my benefit, so we could set course accurately the first time out. Below us were the perimeter lights, a giant bull's-eye. The station beacon flashed "C". Dah-di-dah-dit, dah-di-dah-dit. "C" for home. Sid turned until the compass needle was lined up with the course he had set on the ring. The coast was immediately below us and the moon threw a crinkly shaft of light off the sea.

The pencil track I had drawn across the Channel from Holmsley to Morlaix was ticked off like my pencils: one inch is four miles or a minute. The number of ticks gave me the time to target. We were under strict orders not to fly anywhere near the Normandy beaches where our soldiers and the Brits and Yanks were trying to nail down a bridgehead. We weren't told damn all about Normandy. We had to get our dope from the *Express*. I would have liked to read the *Times* but some Brit liaison officer always grabbed it first. If the Brits saw a Canadian reading the *Times*, they'd think he was trying to put on airs. When I did manage to get my hands on a copy, I always read "In Memoriam" first. This is the column where live Brits agonize over dead Brits publicly. The war was already five years old so that agony was getting longer and longer, if not deeper and deeper.

We droned over the Channel. I could feel in my tunic the compact escape kit, which included some French and other European currency, a map, and a few chocolates. We had left all our personal stuff in the ops room and taken only a photo which showed us in civvy clothes. The object of this gambit was to have a ready-made photo to be used by the French, Belgian, Dutch, or whatever underground to prepare false papers for our daring escapes across the Pyrenees into Spain or across the Alps into Switzerland. Every guy on the squadron had been photographed wearing the same tired civvy jacket, shirt and tie. I could hear a Gestapo gorilla saying to his buddy: "Hey, here's that 418 jacket again, the same one 33 squadron used in 1942. It's getting threadbare."

This kind of speculation occupied a few moments, but didn't serve to take my mind off the coast ahead. Just a duck in for a quick look, then a quick duck out, and that's it for Op. No. 1, I hoped. I started to get jumpy, shifting my feet, examining my map, though there was only the Channel to see.

"Look out the back," Sid said. I craned my neck around and peered out the rear of the cockpit. I was supposed to be looking for enemy fighters crawling up our tail. It was damned embarrassing for interceptors to be themselves intercepted. Sid was always saying, when he couldn't think of anything else, "Look out the back." I still have a bad back and neck.

Time moved on, swiftly, too swiftly. I was going to have to cross that coast whether I liked it or not. We had only a few minutes to go, when we began running into some cloud. We were at 500 feet and I couldn't get anything on the Gee box to show whether we were on track. We were too far from England or Jerry was jamming the Gee or both. I couldn't pick out any blips in the green fuzziness so I turned the box off. Looking at the Gee box was harder than looking out the back. The machine was behind Sid's seat and I had to twist around to get my face into the tube (a face fit neatly into it) to read the screen while I fiddled with the knobs.

"Three minutes to the coast," I said.

Sid began to pull up to 2,000 feet. We had been taught to pull up and then dive across the coast to give us more speed if somebody began shooting at us from the ground. When we got up to 2,000 feet, we were in unbroken cloud.

Sid put us into a shallow dive when I figured we were close to the coast and we entered France for the first time. We didn't see damn all. No France. No Paris. No Morlaix-Lannion. Blanko.

"Shit," Sid said. I had to admit to myself it was a bit of a letdown, on the tourist level alone if nothing else.

We inched down to 800 feet. Still cloud. I thought this was plenty low enough, seeing we weren't sure where we were.

Sid didn't think so. We dropped another couple of hundred and broke cloud. We could see some black countryside.

"Where's the field?" I wondered aloud.

"You don't think they'd light up just because they thought we might be coming," Sid said.

"Might as well go home," I said hopefully.

"Christ, boy, we just got here. We were sent to patrol these two goddam fields for two hours and we're going to patrol them for two hours."

God, what a start to a tour, I thought. Thirty-four more trips with this dead-keen jerk. "Now get cracking," Sid ordered.

I got us turned around and headed back toward the coast. When we got it in sight, we turned port and ran along inland until I could spot a headland which would pinpoint us. Then we did wide circuits around where we judged Morlaix and Lannion must be. The cloud kept crowding us.

"There's the runway," Sid said suddenly.

"Don't get so damn close," I said. "They won't light up

if they know we're lurking about." Lighting up usually meant a plane about to land.

This was only one of many ploys I used to try out to keep Sid far away from their shooters. None of them worked. He wanted to see every bloody thing he could from as close as possible.

Nothing happened this night. No lights came on, even from a farmhouse. No sturdy resistance fighter flashed us an encouraging sign from his secret hiding place. We just stooged around and around and around. The cloud got lower and we were just ducking under it. After an hour and a half of this, I felt bold enough to say: "Let's pack it in."

Sid looked at his watch. "In half an hour," he said. After half an hour, he said: "Give me a course for base."

"Zero-one-five," I told him. I'd had it ready for two hours.

I didn't say anything until I altered the course slightly after peering into my green bag of tricks behind Sid's seat when we were nearing the English coast.

"Check the pistol," Sid said. I looked up the code. Green was the color for the Very pistol between 2 A.M. and 4 A.M. that day. The pistol poked permanently through the roof of the cockpit behind me. You fired it for identification if your own side started shooting at you or began conning you with searchlights. The identification colors changed every two hours.

I reached up, broke open the pistol, pulled out the shell and put it in my lap to look at it. I held the flash in my left hand, cupping the light so that Sid got as little of it as possible. The shell was green, it said. I put it back in the pistol and closed the breach.

"Check the IFF," Sid said. IFF meant Information, Friend or Foe, (as opposed to FFI, which was Free From Infection). I didn't know where the IFF black box was located. All I had to know was where the switch was to make sure it was turned on and sending out a signal that we were friendly, friendly, friendly.

"Check," I said.

"Check the gas," Sid said. I peered at the gauges at my right shielding the flashlight again. "Check," I replied.

The coast came up and there was dah-di-dah-dit. Sid pushed his transmitter button. "Credo two-nine."

"Credo two-nine, this is Grapeshot. OK to land." Grapeshot was code for the airdrome. Grapeshot's voice crackled in my helmet like somebody was walking on walnut shells. It was always the same voice, Bradley's. Gravel Voice, we called him. We would have called him Grapeshot but were warned against breaking secret codes.

Bradley would sit in the blacked-out control tower hour after hour, drinking coffee and smoking. When a Mosquito was late getting home, he'd lean forward on his elbows, his hands clamping his headset more closely to his ears. Nobody else in the control tower dared move. "Shut up, shut up," he'd shout. "There's still somebody up there." I don't think he ever took a night off unless flying was scrubbed because of weather. I was told he'd never taken leave in a year. He never spoke to any of us in the mess. Just a nod at the bar, maybe. I suppose if he had ever addressed us he would have said, "Hello, two-nine."

We did a circuit. Sid put the wheels down and we came into the final approach. "Check your straps, boy," Sid said. I yanked my straps as tightly as I could, which meant I could hardly breathe.

We neared the flarepath. We showed no lights. We didn't want Jerry doing to us what we were trying to do to him: butcher him in his own circuit on his own field.

Sid rolled her on the runway at 140 miles an hour. He always kept the landing speed well over what was required. Another little insurance policy.

"Belly light on," Sid said. He began to laugh. "Do you always hang on tight like that?" he asked.

I looked at my right hand in the dim light. The tips of the four fingers were stuck fast on the one-inch-wide windowsill. I always did that, but it must have been the first time he had noticed. "It gives me a sense of security," I said.

"I thought I did that," Sid said.

He was still laughing and chortling as we taxied in front of the control tower and to our bay, threading between the little blue and amber lights. Hal was there with the flashlights to guide us in. We wheeled around with a last spurt of dust and wind and shut off. What stillness. Even the door being opened from the outside sounded very loud. Hal put up the ladder and I was down it a lot faster than I had gone up.

"Any joy?" asked Hal. This was the standard question when the door opened though the ground crew already knew the answer was "no" because the guns had not been fired and we had therefore not shot at anything. What was far more important to me, nobody had shot at us.

"Not a sausage," Sid said. This was the standard reply in such circumstances. "Hey, boy," Sid said to me, "Show Hal where you hang on while we're landing."

Oh, God, he was going to tell it all over the squadron.

And he did. He told the cook in the little flight shack where we got the post-op treat: liver and one fried egg. He could hardly wait to get back to the ops room where he informed the intelligence officer and another crew which had landed a few minutes ahead of us. The pilot and navigator had a good laugh but I didn't think the navigator laughed as loudly as the pilot. In fact, I thought he was going through the motions and sounds of a laugh to please his pilot. I didn't say anything. If this was the price of flying with a guy who got you back, I was willing to pay.

We made our non-report to the IO. Our "time down" was already on the crew board, phoned over by the control tower. Ben and Doug were not back. But their target field was a lot farther away than ours.

"You go if you want," Sid said. "I think I'll wait for Ben." I suppose he wanted to regale him with an account of how I hung onto the windowledge for dear life.

We smoked and exchanged "Any joy? No," with another crew and half an hour went by.

Sid went to the phone and called Gravel Voice. "What did he say?" I asked.

"He left with his belly light on," Sid said.

"Why didn't the tower tell him?" I asked.

"His transmitter was on send." This meant Ben had told the control tower something before takeoff and had forgotten to switch his transmitter back to receive. Nobody could get through to him.

"Oh," I said. Two mistakes by careful Ben.

After a few minutes, Sid called the control tower again. "Let's go," Sid said to me. "They might have him somewhere else." The white-lettered sign beside Ben's and Doug's names still said "airborne."

I knew and Sid knew that if another field had landed him it would have reported immediately to Gravel Voice. We went back to the barracks and got into our sacks.

When we got up in the morning, we went next door. A corporal was stuffing Ben's things into a kitbag. "What in hell are you doing?" commanded Sid.

"Gathering things up, sir. The room is empty."

That was the last we ever heard of Ben and Doug. No report that they had crashed and been killed. Or taken prisoner. Just nothing. They simply vanished, as if they had never been born.

CHAPTER FOUR

Our second op. was to Chateaudun and Orleans, southwest of Paris. We flew around the Cherbourg Peninsula and entered France at Le Mont St. Michel. This was our usual entry and exit point until the Battle of Normandy was over and the Germans began running toward Germany. I have never been able to see Le Mont St. Michel in peacetime but I got some marvellous moonlight views of it during my time on 418.

"Look at that beautiful castle," I'd say to Sid. This would be on the way home. On the way out, I was too preoccupied with those creepy-crawlies in my guts.

"You're not a flier, you're a tourist," Sid said. I dropped my travelogues after that, though I nearly exclaimed, later, at the beautiful fall colors in Prussia.

On our third trip, we were sent to Melun and Bretigny, two fields just south and southeast of Paris. I offered to go to Morlaix-Lannion again but unfortunately we didn't have our pick of targets at night. Melun and Bretigny, though not as close to Paris as Le Bourget and Villacoublay, were closer to the big red blob of flak than I cared for.

From the master map in the ops room, we navigators

copied the locations of the German defences: heavy and light flak—that is, anti-aircraft guns. I made the flak areas a little bigger than those shown on the ops room wall. Every night when I was working out a flight plan I hauled out my red pencils and added a bit more color to the flak sites.

There is a scene in Joseph Heller's book, *Catch 22*, in which the airmen sneak into the ops room and move their bombing line in Italy farther north so they can show the area has already been bombed and they don't have to fly the next day. It's a funny fictional scene. But it's true.

As the red blossomed on my maps, around all the enemy fields we patrolled as well as Berlin, the Ruhr, Munich, Hamburg, Kiel, Paris, and the like, the space for routes we could use to and from targets became more and more confined. When Sid took a look one night, he said, "At the rate you're going, we won't be able to get into Europe anywhere."

I didn't say anything. He looked at me and immediately realized that that was exactly what I had in mind. He searched interior Germany among the blobs of red. "Ha," he said, putting his finger on a splotch of red which I had dabbed over some remote village in the empty forests between Nuremburg and Munich, "What is that for?"

"Balloons," I said.

"Balloons? What in hell would the Germans have balloons down there for?"

"Secret research site," I said.

"Who told you that?"

"The IO, naturally." The intelligence officer wouldn't be on duty until after we had gone.

Sid smiled. Maybe he realized I was trying to keep him alive as well as myself. But it was another good story for the rest of the squadron, I could see him thinking.

During this conversation, I noticed that a couple of my navigator colleagues were quietly folding up their maps and slipping them into their canvas carryalls or putting them back in their lockers. Here's good news, I said to myself. I'm not he only one whose ass is falling through his underwear with fright.

Sid left. I looked across the map table at Rick, a little Englishman who curled his hair by greasing it and setting it with his tiny fingers. He was holding thumb and forefinger together in the form of a big O. He began opening and closing thumb and forefinger in the classic gesture of fear. If I must explain, the opening and closing O represented the rectum when fright grabbed your insides.

"Never mind," said Rick. "I have a very loose sphincter myself." He came around the table with one of his maps and spread it out in front of me. It was almost as red as mine.

"You missed a spot near Amiens," I said.

"Thanks," he said, filling it in with his red pencil. Well, there are two scared bastards on this squadron, not just one, I thought.

We patrolled Melun and Bretigny without incident. It was cloudy and therefore difficult to make out anything. To my consternation, to put it mildly, Sid decided to go home by going around the east side of Paris and visiting Beaumont, Creil, and Beauvais on the way.

"Somebody else has those fields," I said.

"We'll bring up reinforcements," Sid said.

Beaumont was lit up momentarily. We hung around for fifteen minutes but nothing happened and we headed for Le Mont St. Michel, skirting the south side of the bridgehead.

Suddenly, Sid spotted a light or lights. "Down there," he shouted. Here we were on our third trip and seeing a light for the first time. Sid stuck the nose down, the speed rose and we roared down on the winking lights. It seemed to be a convoy on a back road.

Sid pushed the button. The cannons under the floor pounded, shaking my feet and legs. The machine guns in the nose went off. At the same second, all the lights on the road went out. We were shooting blind. If we made any hits, nothing burned. I looked to my right and could make out some trees—we were below the tops of the trees! By the time we got turned around for another pass, there was just blackness. We couldn't even find the road.

I braced myself to make a slight criticism. "We were a bit low," I said.

"Yes," he said. It didn't stop him, though, from doing it in future.

When we got home, Hal put up the ladder, ran up a couple of steps and stuck his head into the cockpit. "Some joy, eh?" he said.

Sid had to tell him we were firing just for practice. "Oh," said Hal. He was even more disappointed than Sid. All I could remember were those trees off our starboard wing—above me.

Four days later, our regular touring was interrupted by *vergeltungswaffe*, alias the V-1, doodlebug, flying bomb, buzz bomb, robomb and, in Allied code, diver. The first V-1 fell on Britain June 13, 1944. On June 17 our squadron was sent out against them at night and shot down four.

There was nothing very complicated about the V-1. It was a small glider with an engine in it and it was loaded with explosive. Jerry put enough gas in the engine to make it go to London. When the gas ran out, the bomb fell down on whatever—or whomever—was underneath. The thing understandably made the Brits very jittery. It did me, too.

The launching pads were near the French coast from Le Havre to Boulogne. You'd think they would be easy to find and bomb, but they weren't. The only alternative was to shoot them down, preferably over the Channel where they could cause no damage. There was little point shooting them down over England because they were going to fall out of the sky anyway.

So away we went looking for flying bombs. Better than stooging around France, I thought, until I found out we'd be stooging around at 10,000 feet over France waiting for the bombs to appear.

The first night we set out for Beachy Head, from where

we were going to make track for France. Near Brighton, a couple of searchlights snapped on. They picked us up right away. It was blinding in the cockpit.

"Jesus, tell them we're on their side," Sid said, crouching as far down as he could so he could see the instrument panel. This was old hat. I reached around casually and fired the Very pistol. A beautiful green flare shot out. But the searchlights didn't go off as they were supposed to do. Two more stung us with deadly accuracy. Zap!

"For Christ's sake, you must have got the wrong color," Sid barked. He started to take the airplane into contortions to get out of the lights, but then resumed straight and level flight. "They'll really think we're Jerries if we try to get away," he said.

Meanwhile, I was scrambling around looking for the code color chart. I had left the green flare in from our last trip and had forgotten to check the chart.

"C'mon, for Christ's sake," Sid said. This made me doubly nervous. I located the color key in the map box. Then I began searching for my flashlight.

Sid exploded. "What in hell do you want a flashlight for? You can read a ten-cent pulp magazine in here."

The chart said red and yellow for 10 P.M. to midnight. I was so unnerved that I looked at my watch to check the time.

Sid could read me like a book. "It's after ten o'clock and it's before midnight," he roared. Then he added: "If you don't get those lights off, I'm going to go blind." He was really alarmed.

I looked along the rack and couldn't find the right flare. I thought I was going to be sick. I started over. This time I found one, pinched my fingers getting the old one out, thrust in the new one and pulled the trigger. Nothing happened. My God, was there another red-and-yellow flare? I thought not. I pulled the breach open, slammed it again, fired. There was a sound like a fist in a pillow. Two beautiful red-and-yellow lights soared out aft. The searchlights went out like a basement light clicking off.

"Sorry," I said. It didn't seem adequate. Mercifully, Sid didn't say anything. I think he didn't want to betray that he had been scared, too.

The trip was a washout. We couldn't concentrate on anything after that, though it was really a very minor incident. We carried out a two-hour patrol but didn't see anything.

The next night started out the same. I wore the same shoes as I had the first trip. I also peed under the port wing before takeoff. I stuck with these superstitions, though my feet got damn cold sometimes and the ground crew complained now and then about having to tramp around in my wet spots. A superstition is not a real honest-to-God one unless you stick with it through thick and thin.

I think that I had always been impressed by the film in which Clark Gable got in flying trouble the moment Spencer Tracy forgot his habit of sticking his wad of gum on the cockpit before takeoff. I was not particularly superstitious before the war but I have been since. More than the ordinary ones: a black cat crossing your path, breaking a mirror, walking under a ladder. When I struggle out of my high-back rocker, I have to make sure it stops rocking before I leave the room. Never a hat on the bed. Happy is the corpse that is rained on. You name it—I've got it.

We took off, crossed the English Channel and took up station inside France east of Le Havre. We were at about 2,000 feet. "Look out the back," Sid said.

I stayed like that for an hour. There was a real danger, sitting up in the open, that we would draw a Jerry night fighter. "Jesus, there's one," Sid said suddenly. He jammed the throttles forward.

I looked down. Sure enough, there was a red glow, the exhaust of a V-1. It seemed to be moving fairly slowly, poor judgment on my part. We went into a dive to get more speed. The V-1 was ahead of us. In the blackness, of course, all we could see was that small burning sun in front of us. Because the V-1 was smaller than a plane, you had to get fairly close to get in a telling shot.

We were doing more than 350 mph by this time but we weren't gaining. In fact, we were dropping back a bit. In a minute or so, we had to face the truth that the damn thing was running away from us.

"Russ said to go to 10,000," I said. Russ Bannock, our new flight commander, and Don MacFadyen, had worked out some tactics for the V-1. One of Russ's pieces of advice was to climb to 10,000 and wait there for a V-1 launching. The height would enable us to gain our maximum speed of about 400 in a dive. "Look out the back," said Sid. We climbed to 10,000 and stooged around, my neck getting sorer by the minute.

"There's another bastard," Sid said. He banged the throttles forward and stuck the nose down. The sudden dive lifted me up hard against my straps and my guts came up with a thud against my heart. Down we went like a bat out of hell. We wouldn't be too slow this time. We weren't. We went screaming by the bloody thing before Sid could get set for a shot.

We had been warned about this, too. Jerry mixed 'em up. He'd send one over at 500 miles an hour, which we couldn't catch, and then poop off one at 200 miles an hour. Whether this was deliberate or not we didn't know, of course, but it drove us crazy. We climbed back to 10,000 feet; Sid was sore as hell. He took the two misfires as a personal affront to his flying ability.

Another hour went by and we were thinking of doing one more stooge before heading home, when we spotted a third doodlebug. "By God, this time," Sid said.

The speed went up as we went down. I looked at the clock. It read 350 mph. I looked out along my wing. It was flapping like a seagull working in a hurricane. My stomach gave another wrench. Christ, the wings will come off and we'll go straight in. I didn't take any comfort from what had happened to Tony Barker and Gord Frederick, his navigator. They hit the drink so hard the cannons pulled them through the floorboards of the cockpit and clear of the Mosquito. They got into their dinghies and a rescue plane picked them out of the Channel two miles off the Dieppe beaches. It takes all kinds.

Down, down, down. We were gaining some because the fire coming out of the ass end of the V-1 was getting bigger. The Mosquito was screaming in every joint. Sid had both, big hairy hands on the stick. When he began to pull back, I thought the wings would never stand it. But we began to level out and the clock said 400 mph. Sid pulled and pulled and she kept coming out of the dive. I tore my eyes away from the shaking wing and looked ahead. It was just like looking into a blast furnace.

"We're too close," I screamed. I shut my eyes as the cannons began banging away. I was thrown hard against my straps because cannons going off cut down the speed suddenly.

When the explosion came I thought I was going to be dead. The goddam thing went off right in our faces. I opened my eyes and caught a glimpse of things whirling around outside the window. Black things and blobs of smoke.

"I can't see," Sid said.

"OK, boy," I said. "Just keep her like that. You can cut your speed, though." He throttled back. After those hours of darkness, he had been blinded for a few seconds by the flash. Why we hadn't been smashed up by all that flying debris, I don't know. We had flown right through it.

"I got too close," Sid said.

"I noticed," I said. Now that I found myself in one piece and the props still going around, I wanted to laugh and natter and be Jesus H. (for Hannah) Christ in a blue bottle sitting on the mantelpiece. "Boy, I bet we saved the life of some limey in London reading his paper about how all the doodlebugs are being shot down by the ack-ack guns," I babbled.

"Yes, you're quite a little saviour," Sid said. But he didn't fool me. He was pleased he had finally made a score, no matter how small, in his Jewish war against the Germans.

"Well, we got one," was all he said.

"I hope it's the last." That to myself.

"Check the pistol," Sid said. I did, then turned on the Gee box and got a fix on our position. We were nearly home. That stretch at 400 miles an hour had helped speed things up.

I gave Sid a course: "Three-four-eight." Then I checked the IFF and the gas gauges.

"I bet we're all blistered," Sid said. He was talking about the Mosquito.

We drifted in over the coast and pretty soon our circle of lights showed up. He did a circuit and landed and parked. A flashlight bobbed around under my wing, the door opened, a ladder came up and with it a blurred face.

"Where in hell have you been?" asked Hal.

"We got a doodlebug."

"From pretty close," Hal observed.

"That's been mentioned," Sid said.

I climbed down the ladder. Sid followed and took Hal's flashlight and played it on the wings and nose. There wasn't an inch of paint anywhere. The Mosquito was black. No roundel, no number, no letters, nothing.

"What did you do, fly right up its ass?" asked Hal.

"Looks like," Sid said.

The truck with its little dim lights arrived and we rode back to the ops room. Sid reported to the IO.

A few minutes later, Pete came in smoking an enormous cigar. "One ceegar," he shouted, waving his smoke. He meant he had shot down a V-1.

"The son of a bitch," Sid said to me. "What'll he do if he ever shoots down a plane?" He was really annoyed.

The next afternoon, all the crews went around to have a look at our scorched plane and the CO said in the mess, "Don't get too close to 'em." I could have said that.

Sid didn't talk about shooting down a V-1. He talked about mistakes. "Jesus Christ. There we are going down like a stone in a well and my alligator sitting there with his balls in his mouth he's so scared and I'm fingering the old tit to get ready for a shot when we go tearing by as if that goddam thing had stopped to let somebody off. Then my alligator lectures me on tactics."

The bar laughed and roared. "Back up we go, with my alligator twitching like a dry leaf on the end of a dry twig in a dry wind because he's afraid a Jerry is going to come up our ass while we're trying to get up a doodlebug's ass. Well, we spot another, though my alligator here pretends he doesn't see it and says we should go home another way, like the three wise men. Well, down we go again. I don't know how you're supposed to tell how far away you are. I thought we were about 300 yards away when I fired. Jesus, we weren't three yards away. I'm going to wear dark glasses at night after this."

More laughter.

No other pilot talked like Sid did. The others never admitted mistakes. They'd rather die than admit they had, for instance, overtaken a V-1 without getting a shot in. Oh, they had heard about that happening to somebody over in 605 squadron (our RAF equivalent). But that was all.

Except when describing a kill, most crews kept to themselves what went on in the cockpit. I was always interested in how the other navigators got on with their pilots and once in a while I found out.

One said his pilot gave him shit all the time in the air—a constant stream of instructions, complaints, invective about his navigation. But he didn't feel like retaliating because his pilot was so damn good he didn't make mistakes—he knew exactly what he was doing and what his plane could do every second the plane was in the air. It was uncanny. He added that he didn't speak to his pilot except in the ops room and in the plane. This must have taken some doing because, like the rest of us, they bunked in the same room.

Bill told me about his pilot: "Look, he makes mistakes. He puts on the wrong course sometimes. He's not one of your wonder pilots we have around here, with years of instruction.

He made the course and he tries hard and he really flies pretty well. Do you think I'm going to hold him up to ridicule in front of the mess?"

I didn't consider that Sid was ridiculing himself or me. He was simply entertaining the squadron. Besides, he was telling the truth while he did it, with a pinch of exaggeration here and there. I won't say he was the only one who told the truth. But he was the only one who broadcast it.

CHAPTER FIVE

One night, after several V-1 sorties, we were assigned a "flower" to Munich and Ingolstadt. Flower was the code name for our patrols of Jerry airfields when the bombers were out. We were never told where the bombers were going, or how many, or by what route or at what time. We knew only that we were on a flower and, ergo, the bombers were bombing.

This was our longest trip yet. Most of the navigation would be pretty easy because the moon was full and we didn't expect much cloud cover until we were on our way home.

We crossed the coast near Le Tréport. We didn't bother any more to climb up and dive over the coast. We just went in at low level. I could make out the dark patches of wood, though sometimes they were difficult to distinguish from the shadows of passing clouds. In the moonlight, the white strings were roads. The dots and dashes of white were the staccato puffs of smoke from trains. Rivers and streams were silvery and they winked.

My heart skipped once, like a quick dance step, when a searchlight, then another, snapped on. Sid drove on steadily at 500 feet. The lights groped around but we were gone before they could find us. They liked stuff at bomber height.

I watched the ground unfold, picking out the pinpoints easily, a bend on the Moselle, the big bend on the Rhine, a bend on the Neckar, another on the Danube and Ammer Lake. A piece of cake. It was great not to have to worry about the height because of the moonlight. We figured we lost a lot of guys on black nights when they simply ran into the deck.

We were on our final leg to Munich when Sid said, "That looks like a field lit up." It was enough to ruin the evening right then.

The field was probably Argelsried. Sid did a circuit to port at a fairly respectable distance from the field, though it was still too close for me. Then he did another, closer this time. The flarepath remained lit but we couldn't see any signs of activity in the air. We didn't carry interceptor radar like the standard night fighters and a Jerry had to be showing some light before we could see him.

This time around, I peered at the perimeter, trying to make out any planes parked on the ground. Not only did I fail to spot any planes; I couldn't see any hangars or a control tower or damn all. Just woods and a few roads. If we were going to see anything on the ground, this was the night for it. Suddenly, lights showed on the flarepath, moving slowly. It looked like a plane taxiing to the east end for takeoff.

"Here we go," said Sid. He pulled farther away so that he could turn and line up on the flarepath, went into a shallow dive and got his firing finger on the tit.

The moment he fired, all the crap in the world came up at us. My guts dropped right through my ring. I could feel my pants flapping against my legs. This was because my legs were shaking.

Flak is orange and yellow and red tennis balls, coming up in a steady and awesome stream. Every ball seems to come right through the nose of the aircraft.

Sid shoved the speed up and we were through it in a couple of seconds, untouched, apparently. We'd been suckered.

"Dummy," said Sid, speaking of the field, not me. "The dirty bastards," he added.

We hadn't even been thinking of the possibility this far into Germany. And this dummy field was pretty rudimentary. There were none of the fake taxi strips, hangars and perimeter lights some of our guys had run across. Dummy fields were as old as the war.

"We'd better look for the real one," Sid said. After a few more seconds, he said, "What's the course?"

I still couldn't speak. My mouth was opening and closing but the voice box wouldn't work. "Just a second," I finally squeaked.

The map I had been reading was wadded up in a tight ball in my right fist. I smoothed it out as best I could, still holding my flashlight in my left hand. I couldn't concentrate properly and my flashlight searched about wildly for the track I had drawn on the map in the ops room. At last the light hit it accidentally. I figured we were considerably north of our track and guessed at a new course.

"One-zero-zero," I said.

"A nice round figure," Sid said.

For a guess it was pretty good, though. We flew smack over Argelsried, one of the fields we were supposed to patrol. There was a village with a stream running through it, then a wood, and then a bloody runway, a real one. We weren't supposed to start a patrol by doing a run right over the field. We were supposed to approach surreptitiously, though how you could be surreptitious between two roaring Merlin engines was more than I could figure.

"Best navigation you've ever done," Sid said, knowing damn well that flying directly over the field had been farthest from my intentions.

We pulled away a mile or two and began circling the area. We fiddled around for half an hour, my nerve ends slowly ceasing their twanging. If Jerry had gone to the trouble of dragging a dummy plane across a dummy field, we figured there would be some activity with real planes here.

We were about to leave when the lights came on and we got into the circuit, hoping we'd see a Jerry and be able to crawl up his chuff for a shot. But we didn't see anything. After a little while, one burst of flak went straight up from the end of the runway, a warning that there was an interceptor (us) lurking about. We thought Jerry might still have tried to get in, but after a while the lights went out. It was possible, of course, Jerry had sneaked in without us seeing him.

We pushed north to Ingolstadt. Again, the lights were on and we set up a circuit.

"Look out the back," Sid said. I stared at our moonlit tail.

"Let's go back to Munich," Sid said after half an hour. This gave me a chance to unscramble my neck but it threw my flight plan all out. We'd be going home from Munich instead of Ingolstadt, as I'd planned.

We could make out the outskirts of Munich quite clearly. Once in a while, we could see a small glimmer of light from a car or building. How the Poles would have liked this trip.

A Polish squadron was based with 418 at Ford earlier in the year. It hadn't lasted much more than a month. The Poles were assigned targets in France, but decided to hell with the flight plan when they were in the air. Off to Germany they flew. The first light they saw in Germany, they hammered it. They didn't care whether it was a plane, a truck, a train, a farmhouse, or somebody smoking a cigar. They fired until they were out of ammunition. They just wanted to kill one German. If it were more than one, so much the better. But it had to be at least one. Our guys figured the Poles were all shot down by flak or ploughed into the deck. The whole squadron was wiped out. Dave told me that the RAF commander at Ford said in the mess that he didn't care how the Poles flew but that the RAF couldn't stand those kind of losses in new planes.

There was nothing doing at Munich but we hung around until our patrol time was up at 0230.

We hadn't reached the Rhine on the way home, when we

saw a train chugging through some open country. I looked at the map, found the railway track, and saw it was one of the few places on all my maps of Europe not liberally daubed in red. Sid didn't ask my advice. He turned north along the track and we quickly overtook the train. We had been taught to attack a train lengthways, so that if there was an ammunition car or something like that we'd stand a better chance of blowing it up.

This isn't exactly what Sid did. He made the first run over the train lengthways, but he didn't fire straight away. He waited until he had the engine in his sights and then let go with the cannons and machine guns. The boiler blew in a great cloud of steam.

There was nobody shooting at us. Sometimes trains carried a flak car which fired back but this one didn't. The train was stopped and we had it at our mercy.

Sid came round slowly and began coming in broadside. "What in hell are you doing?" I asked.

He didn't say anything. Suddenly a door in one car opened and the light streamed out as one or two people jumped to the ground. "Ah," I heard Sid say. The car with the light streaming out was obviously a passenger car.

Sid raked it with everything we had, cannons and machine guns. He went around again. More doors had opened and more people were jumping out. There were some licks of flame here and there.

Sid poured the shells into that one car. I could see people flinging up their arms or jumping or falling out of the doors. We went around again, came in low and deliberately, with lots of time to get lined up. By now the car was burning fiercely. Sid held down the button as long as he could before he pulled up over the flames. He continued to ignore the other cars. There must have been twenty others.

The flames shot up and, combined with the moonlight, gave us a clear picture of the train. It seemed to be made up entirely of freight cars except for the one passenger car. Though the boiler had blown, the engine was still on the track. I could see a few people lying flat in the ditch near the burning car, but couldn't tell of course whether they were alive or dead. We had stopped the train in the open countryside. There wasn't even a village nearby. There were open fields near the track and woods farther back from the line.

"Let's go round again," I said. Jesus wept, I was part of this, too.

"That doesn't sound like you," Sid said.

He was dead right. If I had to leave home, I was all for getting back as soon as possible. I was the one who sang most often in the bar the words George, another navigator, had put to a famous song: "When the compass course is west, that's the time that I love best."

I think I was just trying to show Sid that maybe terror wouldn't engulf me every time the guns were fired. We went around again. I didn't suggest a lengthways run on the chance we might knock out some ammo cars. We went in the same way, broadside, but using only the machine guns this time because there was little movement we could detect apart from the flames licking away at the car.

Soon after we headed west again we began running into cloud. It got heavier as we neared the Rhine and Sid pulled up to about 3,000 feet. I had to start figuring out what the new height and the wind would do to our course. I changed maps to one nearer home and was looking out to see whether I might get a glimpse of the Rhine through a break in the cloud.

But the cloud got thicker and I noticed an odd, orange tinge to it below us. Must be some odd effect from the moonlight, I thought. Funny that it would be below and not above us, though.

"Dear Christ," Sid said. I looked around but didn't see anything except that funny-colored cloud. "We're right over a target," Sid shouted.

It took me only another second to twig to the news, already known to the Germans, that Wiesbaden was the target for tonight. We were sitting in smoke and that odd hue came from the burning city. If there were still any bombs coming down, they were missing us. The big flak was seeking the bombers high up. There was no low-level flak.

Sid shoved up the speed and we got the hell out of there. "What's your next pinpoint — Berlin?" he said.

The smoke and cloud disappeared — was there any cloud, or was it all smoke? — and Sid started to reduce altitude. Just as he did, the orange tennis balls came up again and two searchlights latched onto us at the first try.

My guts gave a great lurch and then seemed to career about inside my body. My mouth fell open and there was a taste of sloe gin in it. Sid cranked the Mosquito one way and then the other. More geysers of tennis balls shot up toward us and more searchlights snapped on ahead of us. They were going to pass us on, a spotlight sweeping us across a stage.

My hands started to shake and all the maps on my knees slipped to the floor. I tried to grip the floor of the cockpit with my toes.

"How far down can I go?" Sid asked, crouching as far forward as possible to try to prevent the searchlights from completely blotting out his instruments. I couldn't speak. I was fighting just to get my mouth closed because I thought I would vomit up my heart.

"Give me the height," Sid said.

More red, orange, and yellow cataracts streamed toward us and seemed to pass directly between my knees. I decided that if I couldn't speak I might be able to move some other part of my body. I bent over to try to retrieve my maps on the floor but came up hard against the straps. My fingertips brushed against them but I couldn't pick them up. Before I straightened up, I put the heel of my right hand against my jaw and pushed my mouth shut. This stopped the dribbling.

"Can't you speak?" Sid said. With all his other worries, he had managed to diagnose my problem. "I've got to get down," he said.

"Don't go below 800," I said. My voice sounded very high-pitched, but at least I had found it. Even 800 feet was a bit risky because there was a lot of high ground around. But flying low was less risky than taking flak.

There was a sharp crack against the starboard engine and a tongue of flame leapt from it, the slipstream sucking back sparks. We had been hit.

"Quick, boy, the extinguisher." Sid was calm.

A great sheet of flame licked back over the engine cowling only a couple of feet away from me. My finger found the extinguisher button to my right and pushed it. At the same time, Sid pressed the button on the panel which stopped the starboard engine and he pushed the stick forward. My mouth fell open again. I moved my lower jaw back and forth slowly and kept doing that until I got it closed.

The dive helped keep our speed up, even though we had lost an engine. The foam in the extinguisher under the engine cowling had suffocated the fire. The propeller was stopped and one arm stood up like a sentry.

The flak lessened and, suddenly, it was night again. Sid had broken out of the searchlights. Soon there was only some desultory flak behind us.

"Christ, we made it," Sid said. "The bastards thought they got us." I had thought so, too, but I didn't say it. Anyway, I was still having difficulty holding my mouth closed. I was dreading that I would soon have to learn to speak again because I knew the question that was coming.

"What's the course?" That was the question. To stall my reply, I said, "Pull up a bit. We're too low."

Sid pulled back gently on the stick. We were doing 180 miles an hour, the normal speed on one engine. The speed fell off — 170, 160. Sid levelled off again and got the speed back. Then he eased us up another 200 feet.

"Steer two-ninety," I said. "Two-nine-zero."

That was temporary. I had to get my maps back. I lunged against the straps but still couldn't reach them. I stuck out my right foot and dragged all the maps back against my left leg. I got them in my lap. Then I had to sort them out to find the right one.

"You got a proper course?" Sid asked.

I switched on my flashlight.

"Turn off that goddam searchlight," Sid said. He often said that. The flashlight had a round piece of cardboard with a hole in it in front of the tiny bulb and under the plastic end. Only a pinpoint of light escaped. Nearly every afternoon, after Sid's complaints of the previous night, I made the hole smaller. It was so small now I could barely get a needle through it. My eyes would never survive a tour even if the rest of me did.

"Give me a second," I said.

I didn't have the faintest idea where we were. It was important to know because I didn't want to take us over another target for tonight. We had been twisting and turning at high speed trying to throw off the searchlights and avoid the flak. But we had lost speed since. I tried to do some calculations about speed and distance but gave up. What in hell did he want in the cockpit, a mathematician? Anyway, England was a navigator's dream. He just headed west or northwest and sooner or later he hit it.

I figured 290 degrees was too much if we were going to hit Le Tréport on the way out. So I made it 270. That wouldn't do. Too pat.

"Two-seven-two," I said.

"How long before we get to the coast?"

"I'm working on it."

I put my pencil with the ticks along the track and counted off thirty-one ticks. "Thirty-one minutes," I said boldly.

"Don't forget we're doing 180, not 240," Sid said.

I had.

"Yeah, I know," I said. "Well, give it another minute or two."

"I should have dropped you at High Fuckall," he said.

That one hurt. I didn't want to crew up with anybody else. I just wanted to get through this goddam tour in one piece. He might get a better navigator but I didn't see how I could get a better pilot. He could land a plane without an undercarriage, shoot straight, and get out of flak. You couldn't ask for much more, except perhaps for a good, single-engine landing which Sid would have to do presently. Any landing you walked away from was a good one.

We'd been in that cramped cockpit for nearly five hours and we were both getting cranky. "How far to the coast?" Sid asked.

"About four minutes," I said. Sid glanced sideways at me. He didn't believe me but he didn't say anything. I didn't believe myself.

My face was itching like hell from the rubber mask. We didn't carry oxygen — we seldom flew high enough (10,000 feet) for that. But the mask held the intercom. Sid usually left his unhooked so that it dangled at his left shoulder from the helmet. If he had something to say to me, which wasn't very often, he held the mask over his mouth. He pushed up the little button, spoke, pushed the button down again and let go of the mask. This tended to discourage any long-winded conversations, or any conversations at all. He just wanted basic information from me. I kept my mask hooked across my mouth most of the time. Being in a state of nerves all the time, I was all thumbs with the hook and button when trying to put the mask in place. It was easier to have it already in position when my guts fell through my ring. If I survived the war, I'd have piles for the rest of my life. With all the beer, booze, and fright, one would have thought I would have had the loosest bowels in Christendom. I didn't. The appropriate muscles constricted rather than loosened. Perhaps I could unhook the mask and have a good scratch after we were out over the Channel, I thought.

I kept looking at the speed, a steady 180 mph. Then I'd look at my motionless prop, then at Sid's. Keep on turning, wagon wheel.

"Not bad," Sid said.

"What?"

"The coast, right on time," he said. I was even more surprised than he was.

"Look out the back," he said.

I'd been so fascinated by that motionless prop that I'd forgotten to keep my rear vigil. Craning around made my back and neck ache more.

"Twenty-three minutes to the other coast," I said before he could ask me. I looked down at the waves breaking on the French shore. I wasn't sure where we were on the coast but I'd be able to get a fix on our position in a few minutes from the blips on the Gee box screen.

We were forty miles or ten minutes off course. That's OK as long as it doesn't take you over flak sites and trigger their guns. Navigators weren't in a competition for best navigation of the month. The only object was to get to the target and get home again. Particularly home again, as far as I was concerned. Missing a target wasn't going to make me broken-hearted.

I didn't tell Sid we were forty miles off course but he didn't have much trouble figuring it out when I gave him the new course for Holmsley after deep consultation with the Gee box.

"Bit off," he said.

"Oh, a bit," I said airily. Considering everything, I thought I was pretty damn close. Time dragged as we droned across the Channel at 180.

"Credo two-nine," Sid told Grapeshot. "One engine."

"Come straight in," Grapeshot said. The crash truck and meat wagon would be taking their places near the runway.

We didn't make a circuit. We came right in on final approach. Sid rolled her on just as if we had the usual two engines. I gripped the window frame more tightly than usual.

"Nice," I said when the tail came down on the runway.

"I used to fly a Harvard," Sid said. A Harvard has one engine.

Now I knew he could land without an undercarriage, shoot straight, get out of flak, and land with one engine. My part was to learn to get my voice box working when my heart was hammering in my throat. I never did, though.

Sid reported to the night crew chief so that engine repairs could start first thing in the morning, which was only a couple of hours away. Then we reported to a yawning intelligence officer. Then we went home. All other crews were back so there was no immediate listener for Sid's latest story.

That gave him time to polish it up for the next evening in the mess. "Have you heard the latest about my resident genius?" he began. "The shit is coming down on Wiesbaden. And the shit is coming up from below. And guess where we are. Smack in the middle. A couple of tourists rubbernecking around. 'Why, there's a bit of cloud,' says my alligator. And he steers me into the smoke. We damn near smothered to death."

The audience is growing. This is too good to miss.

"What was that?" said a newcomer.

Sid went back to the start, embellishing the tale as he retold it. "Bright moonlight, it is. We take a shot at a train and then start back. My alligator thinks his work is done. 'Home, Charles,' he says. He leans back and starts to read *The Seven Pillars of Wisdom* in the moonlight. I give him a nudge now and then and ask for a course but he says, 'Drive on.' I see this white stuff up ahead and say 'What's that?' He says, 'A bit of cloud. You heard the met man.' Into this cloud we go. It's a fireworks factory. All kinds of colours reflecting through the cloud. There we are, sitting right on top of the goddam target. Bombed by our friends above. Fired on by enemies below. I expected my boy to say, 'Let's stay here a while and enjoy the show'."

I did have a copy of *The Seven Pillars of Wisdom*. I kept it to demonstrate my intellectual prowess and carted it around in my kitbag from station to station. I never did read it. I haven't yet.

Rick was giving me his usual sign with thumb and forefinger. George brought his drink over and sat down beside me. "I did the same thing one night. Over Dortmund."

"I'll never tell," I said.

"Thanks, I wouldn't want to steal your thunder," George said.

Munich was Trip No. 7. We'd reached the magic number. Now it was supposed to be all downhill. This myth, however, didn't account for Jones and MacIntyre, dead on their twenty-eighth; Hare and Stratton, missing and presumed dead on their thirtieth. When you were known dead, as opposed to missing and presumed dead, you got KIA beside your name in the record books. Killed in action. If you were killed, but not on ops, you got KFA. Killed in a flying accident. And DW was died of wounds. If you fell drunk off a tube platform in front of a train, you got KAS. Killed on active service.

In one trip, I had survived two shoot-ups, nesting on a bomber target, and a one-engine return. My cool assessment was that that was about all the ill luck I could have in one trip. I was wrong.

After Munich, we went back on V-1 patrol for a few nights. The CO informed us that a V-1 shot down would be, for the record books, a Jerry plane shot down.

"Shit," Sid said. Whatever the record books might say, he would know the difference: one was a robot, the other a plane with a real Jerry, or Jerries, in it. I didn't feel one way or the other. The pilots got the credit for destruction, and so they should have. If it had been up to me, destruction of anything would have been meticulously avoided.

The CO had more news about the V-1. It chilled me. A V-1 trip would count only as half an operational trip. If a crew did a whole tour shooting only at doodlebugs (nobody did), it would have to put in seventy trips, not thirty-five. I immediately counted up the V-1 sorties and divided by half. I would have to fly three more trips just to get where I already thought I had been. Munich wasn't No. 7 after all. It was No. 5½.

"Think of the shit the bomber boys have to take for a trip," one of the pilots said.

"They have more and better company," I said. Our Lancaster bomber carried a crew of seven.

"And they cruise at 180," the pilot said.

I was too scared for myself to have any sympathy left over for the bomber types, even after I had seen flak blow a bomber apart high above us — the burning pieces had come raining down. "Better him than me," I had said to myself.

I didn't know whether to advise our troops in the Normandy bridgehead to overrun the V-1 launching sites faster so that I wouldn't have to do many more halftrips, or to ask them to slow down so that I wouldn't have to do the even more terrifying full trips.

Sid got three more V-1s. On the first, we got too close again and this time lost an engine.

"Jesus, I guess I'll never learn," Sid told the mess. "My alligator warned me we were too close, but he always says that anyway. He just sits there and screams 'pull up' or 'get back' or 'slow down'. I've never heard him say 'full speed ahead' or 'charge'."

He was right there.

Sid had made another perfect one-engine landing, this time at Ford. We had to wait until the next afternoon before the plane was fixed and that got us out of flying that night though Sid told Bannock we were ready. Well, Sid might have been.

We got another V-1 so fast I didn't have time to be scared. We were just leaving the English coast for our patrol station over France and the Channel when Sid spotted a doodlebug coming at us. We were on a collision course. Sid pressed the firing button and yanked the stick to starboard at the same time. The V-1 exploded and none of the debris hit us.

"What a shot," I said when I got over my surprise.

"Just shows what a little practice will do," Sid said, as if he tried head-ons a couple of days a week.

"They'll never believe it," I said.

"Sure they will. I'll tell 'em you plotted it all the way across on your magic box and gave me the angle and time to shoot."

"But the Gee box can't do that."

"Hell, the other pilots will never know that."

This was the longest conversation we'd ever had in the cockpit. I suggested that maybe we should go back to base to check on any possible damage.

"You never change, do you?" Sid said, and took us up to 10,000 feet, keeping course for France.

We were stooging back and forth along the coast when the engine began to sputter and we suddenly dropped.

"Gas!" Sid yelled.

Christ, I'd made another boner. After we took off, we switched to the drop tanks to use up the gas in them first. Ordinarily, we took the drop tanks home with us, but if we needed a bit more speed we could easily jettison them with the push of a button.

I always watched the gauges carefully and switched back to the main tanks just before the gas in the drops was used up. This time I had forgotten to switch. We were temporarily out of gas.

I grabbed the fuel cocks and turned them. Sid put the nose down and we were dropping like a lead weight. The engines coughed and coughed, then caught while my blood drained into my shoes.

Sid took us back to 10,000 feet. After a while, he said, "I suppose you know what would have happened if we had been at 500 feet."

"Yes." We would have gone straight into the deck, never to be heard of again. Only our height had given us a chance to recover.

We were home early because we'd left early. That meant we'd be seeing a good many of the other crews. Sid started back at the beginning. "I think all of you have met my boy, here, McIntosh, from Quebec. We met at High Fuckall. We come back from map-reading and our station is flashing Y and the one next door is flashing K. My boy, here, thinks High Fuckall just forgot and dropped the last dash off Y and we land. It's a troop transport station and the tower won't let us take off till the next day. Almost the next night, the undercart won't come down, he pumps for an hour to get it down, and we land with it still up. I should mention in passing that I boiled over the rads and stripped the brakes. They weren't going to let us leave that station, ever. But I signed a paper that I'd get McIntosh through a tour if it killed me. It almost has and we've barely started. Now I don't like to repeat myself, but this is what has happened so far."

Then he took his delighted audience through our repertoire: a Mosquito with all the paint burned off, suckered by a dummy field, sitting on top of the target for tonight, now this little business of forgetting to switch tanks. I must say he didn't spare himself about the dummy field. Everybody was grinning.

"Well, after this thing about the gas tanks," Sid said, "I've been thinking I should write to High Fuckall and ask for that piece of paper back."

"Your boy gives us a lift," George said to me.

"Yeah," I said.

"Do all those things really happen?" George asked.

"Yeah," I repeated. The embellishment I left to my driver.

An even stranger thing happened a couple of nights later when we were on V-1 patrol again. We were about to come home when we could hear, clear as a bell, "Mayday, Mayday, Mayday." This was the distress call. You needed a course home or you were about to ditch in the sea and wanted somebody to come and pick you up, or at least look for you. The call was so distinct that we thought the plane must be in our immediate area.

"Get a fix in case," Sid said. We always collected stray bits of information like this in case they might be useful to someone.

I switched on the Gee box and plotted our position about mid-way in the Channel.

"Get out, you goddam idiot," was the next thing we heard. Then "Mayday" again.

Then a hell of a racket which drowned out the voice in the other plane. This noise reached a very high pitch, then tailed off. The voice cut in clearly again: "Get that goddam door off and get the fuck out."

The transmitter was jammed "on" and we were getting the program direct from the cockpit of the other plane. We could hear a banging and then the noise went up again.

"It's a Mosquito out of control," Sid said.

We waited for the sudden silence, which would mean the plane had gone into the Channel at full bore. But the noise of the other's engines gradually lessened as the Mosquito climbed again. The voice again, screaming: "Get out, get out."

The navigator was obviously having trouble getting the door off. Maybe the handle was stuck and he was sitting on the floor, trying to kick the door out. The navigator's helmet was off or his voice button was pushed to "off" or something. Anyway, we couldn't hear him. Thank God.

Down the Mosquito went again. And back up it came, the pilot still screaming, his voice nearly gone it was pitched so high: "You goddam stupid son of a bitch." Then there was some raspy breathing, as if the pilot had jumped on top of the navigator and was trying to kick the door himself.

Down the Mosquito went again with a roar. Then there was nothing. We looked all around but didn't see anything.

"Jesus," Sid breathed.

I didn't say anything, but I didn't think much of the way that pilot had described his navigator. I got another fix and we went home.

Before Hal could open the door, I got down on the floor of the cockpit and grabbed the handle. It turned OK.

"You don't have to open up," Hal said as he was putting up the ladder.

"That time we did," Sid said.

We told the IO what had happened and gave him the fixes. The Mosquito wasn't from our squadron. We asked the next day about the plane. The usual outcome: haven't heard a thing.

One of several things could have happened. The pilot could have regained control. Pilot and navigator could have gotten out and been rescued or they could have gone straight into the drink. Or, the pilot could have kicked in the head of his navigator, kicked open the door, jumped (leaving the navigator there), gotten into his dinghy and been rescued the next morning. The last was, I judged, the most likely theory. But we never found out.

CHAPTER SIX

We got one more V-1, uneventfully. When you put our total of four against the full statistics — the Germans launched 5,430 V-1s which killed or injured 23,400 people and destroyed or damaged one million dwellings — it doesn't seem like much. And it isn't. Even the squadron figures are small: eighty-three destroyed during 400 sorties. But we felt at the time that we were doing something useful. And the pilots never had better sport. There was no ass-end Charlie shooting back at them from the doodlebug. If one had to go to war, this was the best place for it: above a flakless English Channel with well-lit targets provided by the other side.

Before I joined the squadron, a Jerry intruder just missed picking off one of our planes over Ford and, in a snit, dropped, it was found by later count, eighty-six anti-personnel bombs. There was complete panic. Fearing a German invasion, the officers immediately ordered the ground crew to dig rifle trenches. Once they were dug, the officers jumped into them and told the erks to keep a close watch. Nobody moved until bomb-disposal people had completely cleared the field twenty-four hours later. Even then, there was one hell of a lot of tiptoeing around. The air force just wasn't cut out for this commando stuff.

I was patronizing Hugh Hill, an army friend back from the Normandy battles, on just this point one day when we met in London. "At least when I'm shot at I can run away at 400 miles an hour," I said, referring to the Mosquito's top speed.

"Hell, that's nothing," said my infantry friend. "You should see me."

A stray V-1 arrived at our field one night. We were sitting around in the B flight shack, when the tannoy (public address system) came on and a calm voice from the control tower announced: "We have just been advised that a V-1 is approaching the vicinity of the field. You will be told in plenty of time in case it is necessary to take shelter." Just then, the enormous flame of a V-1 appeared over the trees at the far end of the field.

"And here comes the fucking thing now," the tannoy screeched. Calm Voice in his panic forgot to switch off the mike and we could hear tables and chairs going over in the control tower and the pounding of heavy boots down the stairs.

The V-1 hit an empty hut and nobody was hurt.

Just a few days before the V-1 launching sites were overrun by the army, the Germans began their retreat across the Seine.

"You're going to bomb tonight," our flight commander, Russ Bannock, told us just before we left the ops room for our night flying test.

"Bomb?" I squeaked. I didn't want anything to do with the filthy things.

"Yes," Russ said. He had already shot down eighteen V-1s and three planes and had a brave navigator, Bob Bruce, and didn't understand the concerns of ordinary mortals like me.

"We don't know how to bomb," I said. Russ laughed. He thought I was kidding.

"I do," said Sid. Hero could never keep his big mouth shut.

"It's a nice change from routine," Sid said as we walked toward the plane for the daily test run. But my knees were already shaky. Just thinking of a bomb riding in our plane gave me the cold hand on the scrotum.

Sid told Chiefy the good news, but he already knew, of course. Chiefy was squat, wide, red-haired, and the boss of all the ground crew.

"Yep, a little 500-pounder," Chiefy said.

This didn't sound very little to me but Sid said the two-man Mosquito was often carrying a 4,000-pound cookie to Berlin, the same load as the seven-man Lancaster.

"Why don't they let the Mossies do all the bombing and forget about the Lancs?" I asked.

"I've often asked myself the same question," Sid said.

None of these things was ever explained. Butcher Harris didn't give a damn how many men he lost as long as he was pounding the shit out of German civilians. Butcher was the deserved nickname of the RAF chief of Bomber Command. An air force twin for Haig of the Somme, Ypres, and Passchendaele. One thing about Harris, though, he played no favorites. He was just as willing to sacrifice Brits as Canadians.

"You want to see your little bomb?" Chiefy asked.

"Sure," Sid said.

"Well, we'll have her ready just as soon as you come back."

We were back in twenty minutes from the night flying test and Chiefy and a couple of his boys wheeled the bomb out on a cart. Chiefy was right. It didn't look very big. Chiefy and Hal and another guy trundled the thing under the open bomb bay doors of the Mosquito and wrestled it into place with the help of a couple of pulleys. The operation didn't look very scientific to me but the squadron didn't do much bombing. I kept well back.

We took off gingerly for the Seine as soon as it got dark. We thought we saw some convoys but all their lights winked out before we could pinpoint them on a road. Even for me, it didn't take long to find the Seine, then we went up the river toward Paris until we saw a bridge. It was a dandy great big cantilever bridge. Even better, it didn't seem to be defended. At least there wasn't any flak. We crossed over to the right bank and Sid did a wide circuit to get lined up.

"Just a practice run first," he said. We ran along the length of the bridge, about 500 feet above it.

Sid said he thought he could do better. He went around again and did another practice run. By this time, a Jerry regiment could have fled across it. On the third run, Sid said, "This is it, boy."

He allowed for lead time and everything else in the book. We were dead over the bridge, slow speed, bomb bay doors open, bomb fused. Sid pushed the bomb release. I looked back, expecting to see girders and roadway flying through the bomb-lit night. Instead, the damn thing squibbed off in a field on the far bank.

We never carried another bomb.

We went back to strafing, and one night we hit a convoy near Rouen. One of the vehicles blew up so violently it was above us for a split second. Sid later related to the mess: "It was a jeep. I looked up and there was this goddam burning jeep — above us. I was getting ready to shoot it down when I see the driver hook on a parachute and jump. He got down without a scratch."

Sid was so enthused by this attack on the convoy — we figured we got several trucks — that when we landed back at base with our ammunition all used up he told Hal: "Load her up. We're going out again."

Two trips in one night!

"I have a headache," I said to Sid.

"I won't fire the guns so loudly next time," he said. What a card.

There was nothing for it; he insisted and we went up again, back across the Channel, into France, looking for Germans on the run. And we found some more, shot up another convoy, spent all our ammunition. Once you could start a fire, it didn't have to be a large one to act as a beacon. It gave you time to turn around and line up for another run and, more important, showed the height of the ground. Once we had a blaze going, I could give up shouting at Sid, "You're too goddam low. We're going to hit the deck."

When we got back the second time, I said, "It's nearly dawn." I thought he might have ideas of repeating his fill-'er-up order to Hal.

"I get you," he said.

Hal said, "We'll have to start painting little trucks on the side to show all the convoys you've shot up."

"No," Sid said, quite sharply.

As we walked over for our liver and egg, Sid said: "I don't mind a swastika up there for a plane, but we're not having anything else up there for that other crap." By other crap, he meant V-1s and trucks and trains and anything else on the ground that moved and he could shoot.

That was OK by me. And no swastika at all suited me too.

We got seven days leave every six weeks and always intended to see Britain. Yessir. That Loch Lomond. And all those cathedrals. And the Lake District, absolutely beautiful. And apple time in Somerset. The trouble was, we never saw any of those places or things. And the reason was that to get anywhere in Britain you had to change trains in London. We'd duck down to the Chez Moi for a couple of drinks while waiting for the next train. And there went another leave passed entirely in London, in fact within a few blocks of Piccadilly Circus.

The Chez Moi was a basement bar halfway down Denman Street, a little side street starting at the Regent Palace Hotel. It was the hangout of Canadians in Fighter Command. Across the street was the Crackers Club for Bomber Command. There was little mixing because as far as we were concerned we were fighting two different wars. Flying fighters had nothing in common with flying bombers. Though we were out trying to shoot down fighters while the bombers were bombing, we never visited a Canadian bomber base. No bomber boys ever came to our base. The men of 418 were especially lonely (and proud of it) because the squadron was the RCAF's only intruder squadron. As we drank we told and retold our innumerable and familiar stories of the war, and never seemed to tire of them. Few women came into the place. The only woman around regularly was Old Sylvie who acted as barmaid while she drank up the profits and played a drunken piano for glasses of gin until she fell over and was carried away to a little cubbyhole in the back.

A hotel room in London was never a problem for 418. We nearly always stayed at the Regent Palace. There was a pleasant but very fat and very middle-aged woman who worked the night reservation desk. She was always looking, not in a vulgar way but with discretion, for a lay, but she could never find even a drunken soldier to oblige. One night a 418 member, desperate for a room, pleaded with her for help. She managed to get across her message: no fuckee, no roomee. In a masterstroke of Christian charity, this gentleman pilot agreed to service her if his mates could get hotel rooms on demand late at night. The booze-laden password, "418," huskily whispered through the grill of the reservation desk at the Regent Palace, provided the squadron with rooms for many months while fuming Yanks waving five-pound notes were turned away. The arrangement ended when our brother's keeper was shot down, though we managed to keep the news from our friendly night clerk for some weeks with a story that our stud had been sent on temporary assignment to the far north of Scotland.

Sid was always inordinately lucky at the Regent Palace. He not only got a room but nearly always one on the ground floor just off the main bar-lounge. He could sweep the lounge with a glance as if he were peering from the cockpit for an FW-190. Zap. He could always pick out the service girls on leave who were wearing their old civilian clothes and trying to look like women again. He seldom even had to buy them a drink or, if he did, it was usually a shandy, that ghastly combination of beer and ginger ale. Not because he was tight. He wasn't. It was just that the girls he picked drank, like himself, very little or not at all. They preferred other activities. If he liked the girl at the first go, she could stay all night. If he didn't, she departed and he selected another from the wide variety spread before him in the lounge, like candies in a showcase. One night he brought this Scottish doll back to the room off the bar-lounge we were both purportedly occupying.

"Get up and get dressed," Sid said. "We need the room."

"I'm tired of being a virgin," Scottish Doll said.

"We're both tired of you being a virgin," Sid said.

She was all peaches, cream, and heather, tipsy and dewy-mouthed. Christ, why did Sid have all the luck.

"Where am I going at this hour of the night?" I complained.

"Maybe you can visit my friend upstairs," Scottish Doll said, mentioning a room number on the seventh floor. Sid was already unbuttoning her blouse with one hand and unlacing his shoes with the other.

Probably some cow, I thought. But who was I to carp? Besides, all the pubs, bars, lounges and other drinking establishments were closed and I'd have to mope around the wet streets where the whores laid in wait for boozed-up Canadians and soaked them £5 for a five-minute bash, including foreplay, in a parked taxi just around the corner and up the alley. In the blackout, they could have your cock in one hand and be hefting your wallet with the other before you had time to say you were a nice Canadian boy without any need to rely on whores.

I went up to the seventh floor and knocked on the appropriate door. A blonde vision in a gossamer nightgown immediately opened the door. "What kept you so long?" she said. By God, Sid didn't have all the luck after all.

Unless they were already registered themselves, it was tough getting girls into London hotel rooms. The hotels would close all doors at night and leave one narrow opening, at which was posted a wise old bellman who kept intoning, "Residents only, please, residents only." Nooners were tough, too. If a girl got into an elevator, a wise old lift operator would say, "Are you a resident, miss?" If she said no, the operator said she would have to be met in the lobby. If she said yes, the operator would say, "May I see your room key, please?" All this so unnerved willing but nice girls that they fled in confusion, feeling that in future they would not aspire to a hotel bed but would be content with the usual haystack in the farmer's field at the far side of the airdrome.

It was possible to meet girls in the pubs. But the best place was the Palais de Dance in Hammersmith at the end of the underground. But it was no place for a slowpoke because the last train back to the West End was about 2220 and if you didn't make it you had to dig deep for the price of a cab, if you could find one. The best scheme of all, of course, was to bring your girl with you from the airfield, or whatever, if she'd come. A lot of girls didn't want to because the Brit hotels were murder on shacking up — they seemed to have one house dick for every five rooms — and they also cast a very jaundiced eye on visiting from room to room. It's a wonder to me how the Brits ever reproduced themselves in sufficient quantity to sail the world and populate their colonies with administrators.

A great drawback to wartime London, apart from the Jerries being frequently overhead, was getting something to eat. You had to queue up everywhere and if you were lucky you got beans on toast and then managed to grab the waiter's

Sid and I posing for an official photograph after we returned from our raid on Kolberg.

A Mosquito in camouflage paint. Camouflage, hell.

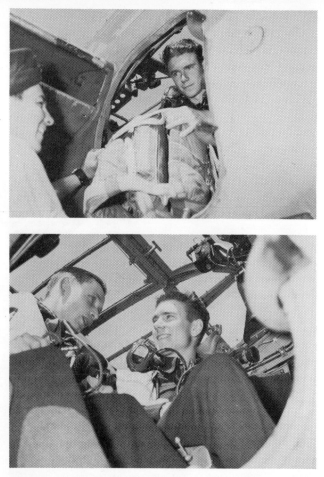

Once pilot, navigator, and their war impedimenta were stuffed into the Mosquito cockpit, there was still lots of room – if you did no more than inhale and exhale. Long confinement in this office was not conducive to an atmosphere of fellowship but led, rather, to hours of silence punctuated by pilot-navigator bursts of crankiness, bitchiness, cursing and personal invective. In these two photos, Corporal T. R. Grimes crams aboard the parachute-dinghy of the pilot, Flying Officer F. A. Johnson, and Johnson flashes a typical pilot's for-camera-only smile at his navigator, Pilot Officer E. J. Gent. The latter looked fifteen years old and was actually, I think, fourteen.

Sid and I being interviewed after some incredible feat of daring (all his). Note Sid's Canada-USA shoulder flash. Some desperately vital information on the wall map has been blanked out to keep it from prying Jerries.

Sid and I posing in front of our Mosquito. The four machine guns project from the nose; the cannons are located behind Sid at head level.

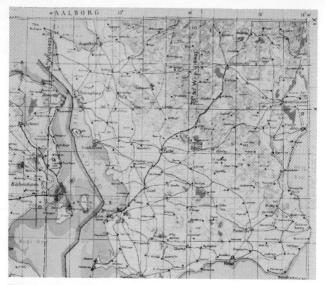

The most tempting map in my wartime collection: Malmo, in neutral Sweden, was only a stone's throw from Copenhagen across the Sound. This map shows Vaerlose just northwest of Copenhagen where Sid and I made our first daylight intruder sortie.

Sid sticks his head out of starboard (my) side of the canopy for this hammy shot of his dog and another pilot. I had to carry the goddam dog on my lap, one of the many extra services provided by navigators for their pilots.

The plotting table in the operations room. Here we worked out courses to get us to target but, far more important, home again.

An example of wartime RCAF publicity (it hasn't improved): my two buddies and I at Air Observer School, Malton, were competing for a sweater of American movie actress Ann Sheridan. She was, for obvious reasons, known as the Sweater Girl.

418 Squadron pennant. The original badge was a Mosquito in flight.

It took me more than a year to get the hat to droop in just this professional manner. A friend of mine, Razor Gillette, drilled a hole in his vizor so he could hang his hat on a nail. In a crowded mess he could always spot his hat, hanging in a different direction from anyone else's.

Sid and his wife, Gail, in Koror, Palau, Caroline Islands, 1965. This was his plane and he also had a jeep and a sailboat and the world by the tail.

arm in time to stop him from pouring the inevitable custard sauce over the already ghastly pudding. Any restaurant to us was a gag-and-puke.

For one leave, I thought things might improve at least gastronomically if I played the part of a limey. When I was in college, I had a sharp Harris tweed suit my mother had bought for me at Rosenbloom's in Sherbrooke. I hated to part with it and packed it around with me in the air force. I decided to try it out for the first time on a London leave. The guys in the Chez Moi thought I was queer, our word for gay. The women thought I had consumption or a wooden leg or a wide yellow streak (only the last was accurate). And the waiters treated me worse than ever for not eating my horrid trifle with repellant custard with a spoon as well as a fork. The worst thing of all was that Sid was ashamed to sit beside me in the Temple bar. "Christ, I'm not going to be seen with some limey faggot with custard all over his pants," he said. I never wore the suit again until after the war, and by then it had become mildewed in the bottom of my kitbag.

I was no tourist. I didn't see St. Paul's or the Tower of London or the Houses of Parliament. But I didn't spend all my waking time in the Chez Moi. Sometimes I went to the Sussex bar off Leicester Square but a lot of the time I went to the theater — the Legitimate Stage, as my mother called it.

London was more nourishing than the Haskell Opera House at home, Lakewood, or the Royal Alex and Hart House in Toronto. I saw everything. Deborah Kerr, Robert Donat, and Edith Evans in Shaw; Jack Buchanan in one of those awful English musicals; Cyril Ritchard, Madge Elliott, and George Graves in *The Merry Widow*. I had the great fortune to see Sid Field in *Strike a New Note* and, later, in *Strike It Again*, with that ravishing dish, Zoe Gail. Whatever became of her?

I still have the program for *The Merry Widow* at the Haymarket. It says in small type at the end: "In the event of an Air Raid Warning an announcement will be made from the stage. Patrons are advised to remain in the Theater, but those wishing to leave will be directed to the nearest official air raid shelter, after which the performance will be continued for so long as is practicable. Should any news of particular interest be received during a performance it will be announced from the stage at the end of the succeeding scene or act of the play."

Other theaters did not even concede the possibility of the performance being ended by an air raid. A wartime program of the Prince of Wales Theater which I have states: "Those desiring to leave the Theater may do so, but the performance will continue." In other words, anybody who leaves is chicken. Luckily, I was never faced with making this decision. It might have lowered the British public's morale if a Canadian airman had been seen as the sole evacuee bolting from the theater. It wasn't hard to pick out a Canadian from other uniforms. We all wore Canada shoulder flashes.

My favorite wartime play was Terence Rattigan's *Flarepath!* I saw it again and again. It was all about a bomber pilot cracking up — mentally, that is — in the middle of his tour. The sound effects and lighting were marvellous: guns, bombs, fires, searchlights. When the house lights came up, I always strolled out casually to show everybody that, by God, the Brits might crack up under pressure but Canadians didn't.

Theater hours were early during the war. With careful plotting, I was able, once or twice, to take in three shows on a single Saturday: an early matinee, an early evening performance and a late evening show. This operation depended on proximity of theaters and a pocketful of sandwiches. I never had the courage to order tea served in my seat between acts. I always imagined the waitress would forget to come back and leave me with the tray and dishes until the next intermission.

I suppose the Brits resented us taking the best seats (which were very cheap) just as they naturally resented us swarming the pubs, but there were always good seats to be had, even at the last minute, except for the musicals which nobody with any taste would attend anyway.

At the end of our first six weeks on the squadron, Sid and I declared to each other we were not going to London. Instead, we would take a Lord Nuffield. This rich Brit nobleman paid the hotel (excluding bar) bills for aircrew on leave. We hunted up the most expensive hotel outside London and settled on the Imperial in Torquay on the Devon coast. No taking the train east to London to come back west to Torquay. We'd go by car.

And we did. Small cars were all the rage on the squadron, and we picked up a Morris Minor from a limey crook for only an arm and a leg — each. There were two big wartime troubles with cars: a shortage of batteries, a shortage of gas. Both were easily solved. If your car didn't start, you simply lifted up the floorboards of a neighbouring car in the squadron parking lot and helped yourself to its battery. The last guy out of the mess who wanted to drive his car was out of luck. Batteries passed from car to car like water pails from hand to hand at a rural fire. It wasn't considered cricket to lock your car. Most couldn't be locked anyway.

There was always lots of gas in the bowsers, the trucks which supplied aviation fuel to our planes. We didn't use av gas, but the truck gas. All you needed was a rubber hose for syphoning and a little stealth. It wasn't considered good form to go crashing about and waken the service police. They were already overburdened hounding tired and broke erks getting in thirty minutes late from a seventy-two-hour pass.

There is a trick to syphoning: when the flow starts, get the hose out of your mouth before the liquid arrives. I think that during the war I swallowed more gas than booze, which is a lot of gas.

We stole enough gas and jerry cans to make Torquay and back. It was a lousy leave. But it was great for Sid. The first night he met this gorgeous thing. She was tired of her husband and had left him back in Bournemouth. She was staying at the hotel. I didn't see Sid again except at meals, when he'd smirk and wave from a distant (and choice) table.

For leave, I never deserted the Big Smoke again. Nothing

could compare with Sid Field, *Flarepath!*, the Hammersmith Palais de Dance, the Tartan Dive at the Sussex, shooting bullshit in the Chez Moi and quick feels in the crowded, blacked-out streets. Just for a second, it took your mind off the fact you'd have to survive ten more trips before you got another leave.

When the squadron moved, Sid and I had to move a Mosquito, of course. One of the ground crew drove the car but the generator was shot and he couldn't get up a hill. So he ran it off into the woods and hid it under brush, just as a lot of us had been taught at a commando course. He marked the spot carefully on the map but when Sid and I went back to retrieve it a week later, we couldn't find it though we beat the bushes for hours. It may be there to this day. Even after thirty-five years it couldn't be much more rusted than when we had it.

The squadron moved to Hurn, also in the Bournemouth area, but there wasn't enough room for everybody so in two weeks we moved again. This time it was to Middle Wallop but it turned out the field was grass and gravel and the wheels kicked stones through our own tails when we took off.

We moved yet again. I was glad to get away for two reasons. We lost an engine soon after takeoff one night and nearly crashed. Even more terrifying were the RAF women officers, cool, beautiful, and disdainful of colonials.

And so we arrived at Hunsdon, a small village with one pub (there had been two but some dumbbell had landed on the other with his plane) only thirty miles north of London. The main railway line to London was only two miles from the field and the station stop was Stanstead Abbot which, I thought, would be good luck for somebody from Stanstead, Quebec. There was a brewery only ten miles away. With such amenities and proximity to London, who would ever need leave?

"All set, fellows?" The flight commander had come into

the ops room at Hunsdon and was addressing the new crew.

"Yes," said the pilot promptly but I could see they weren't. They looked like me, Neverready the Nervous. The pilot was the youngest I'd ever seen on the squadron, maybe nineteen, probably eighteen. And his navigator looked fourteen, though by law he had to be older. They were poring over a map on a small wooden table in one corner. As a squadron veteran, I should have been feeling very superior. But I didn't. I felt sorry for them, which is to say I felt sorry for myself. I was twenty-two, nearly twenty-three, but God, these were babies.

The rookie crew went to their locker and began fishing out Mae Wests, dinghies, parachutes and harnesses while the flight commander stood near the stove, looking at his watch. All thumbs, they fumbled into their heavy life preservers. They buttoned them down the front and passed the hanging cords under the crotch, tying them at the hip.

" . . . and remember at the coast to give yourself three or four minutes so you can climb to 4,000 feet and dive over . . . if you're not sure where you are going in don't go but come back and make sure and go in at the right place once you're in you're OK and make sure of your pinpoints at the end of each leg before you go any farther there's no use going all the way in there if you don't know where you are when you get there and you'll just flog over some place that'll take a crack at you . . . " The flight commander droned on, meaning well, but unheard.

The new pilot picked up his combined dinghy and chute. His navigator was having trouble with his harness and Sid got up to help him with it. The navigator said thanks and gathered the harness straps in front of his stomach where he clicked them, one by one, into the aluminum master lock. He picked up his dinghy and chute, put them down, went over to the table and gathered up his maps, pencils, and compass computer and put them into a haversack. He slung this over his left shoulder as if he'd left the ops room a hundred times and then went back to the locker and picked up his chute and dinghy again. He started for the door, stopped, felt in his haversack. We all tried not to look. Again he put everything down and went back to the locker.

"Can't see my way without a flashlight," he said.

Nobody spoke. Jack leaned over, opened the stove door and tried to stir the damp fire into a token of life.

The navigator rooted about at the bottom of his locker, produced two flashlights, put them in his bag, took them out and tested them, put them back, gathered up his paraphernalia for a third time. The pilot opened the door.

"Good luck," said Sid. It was more than we got on our first trip.

A swirl of early night air scudded into the room. A bar of light cut across the wet ground outside and then the door banged shut. The flight commander stood looking at the door where they had gone out.

"Skip, why don't some of us get these early trips?" Jack said. "Those guys will be back before midnight."

"I'd just like to see you get some trips, early or late," the flight commander said. "You haven't been out for a week."

The weather had been foggy. When it had cleared the odd night, Jack and George were off duty — we worked two nights on, two off. If flying was washed out your second night on duty, you had three nights off in a row. This permitted you to get plastered and still have two nights to get your strength back. You could have a two-day drunk, but I found it risky leaving only one night for recovery. If I was going to get the chop, it wouldn't be because I was hung over. I made enough mistakes as it was.

In a few minutes a plane roared away and the phone rang. The flight commander went into the cubbyhole that was the intelligence room and picked it up. Beside the name of the new crew he wrote, on the blackboard behind the desk, the time of takeoff.

All the crews were smoking. A little heap of butts lay near the heel of each man and around the navigation table and there were more scattered about the stove where they had been thrown without any particular aim.

Jack looked at the crew board and said to the flight commander: "My God, you gave them V Victor. A wing's ready to fall off, I forget which this time."

"If you're afraid of the plane, OK, but don't alarm everybody else." Well, here we go, I thought. Another round of this pilot repartee.

"Afraid?" said Jack. "Just because I had a fire behind my seat and an engine runaway? It's a jinx."

"It may be a jinx but it has six planes to its credit, which is a hell of a sight more than you have."

"My record will improve," said Jack, who had one kill. "I now have the fastest kite on the squadron."

"Like hell you have," said Pete. "I can cruise R at 265."

"With Mickey out in front pulling it."

"Why not? He's pulling it all the time."

There were a few snickers. Whatever the talk, it was better than brooding about the night ahead. Conversation, no matter how inane, was a buffer against the constant disquiet, jumpiness, or outright fear.

I looked at the crew board. I had forgotten to put down our vital statistics. I got my log (form 433A) off the navigation table and filled in the times under the headings: time out English coast; time in enemy coast; time on target; time off target; time out enemy coast; time in English coast; name of target; duration on target; total time; estimated time of arrival at base. Two other entries would be made by somebody else: time off and time down.

I sat down again beside Sid. It was so damp I kept my nonsmoking hand in my pocket, in my tunic under an arm or between my legs. When it got a bit warm I'd switch my cigarette to it and try to warm the other hand. The coke in the stove would never burn properly. It smoked, but luckily most of the smoke went up the stovepipe and outside. Once in a while when somebody would feel like moving around, he'd pick up the dilapidated broom and sweep up the butts. There was always a good crop.

George was the only one not smoking. I wondered how he could be so calm. But maybe he wasn't. We'd all thought Morgan was a cool cookie, too, until he had suddenly left the squadron. Even then his pilot hadn't said anything. But word had got around. Morgan pretended he was lost the moment he got inside the French, Dutch, or Belgian coast. He made his pilot circle and circle, then announced it was just no use, they were lost and might as well go home. Maybe you could do it once or twice, but never every time. One day, he was gone. We never heard of him again. I could understand Morgan's point because my objective was not to win the war but to survive it.

"The heavies took a beating that night," Bill was saying. He was big and blonde and his navigator, Jim, was big and dark, and the women stormed them. I hadn't been paying any attention to the conversation. I'd been trying to think, as usual, of a better pinpoint on the Moselle.

"We were quite near Frankfurt on our way home. It was burning like hell, but the bombers were going down like bloody flies. One poor bastard got it right over the top. Two guys got out and they held them in the lights all the way down. I heard in the Crackers Club the other day what the Jerries do with our guys that get down. They throw them into the fire."

"That makes up for what you did in the Baltic," Sid said.

Bill and Jim and another crew had gone up there in daylight a few weeks before. Five training planes were stooging around over the sea. Bill got two and the other pilot got two. The fifth Jerry ditched and the crew crawled out on the wing and held up their hands. Bill got four of them with his machine guns and the fifth jumped into the water. Jim didn't speak to me about it — and I didn't speak to him about our shoot-up of a train's passenger car.

Bill didn't make any bones about it. "What the hell.

They might have been up shooting at us the next day." He leaned back and added, "Just like flies on a ceiling."

Sid said, "I'm not preaching. All I meant was an eye for an eye."

"Christ, everybody does what Bill did," Tommy put in. "We're supposed to kill Germans. The manual doesn't specify how you do it. I stopped a train not long ago on a ranger (a daylight trip). The engineer jumped out and ran for the woods. I got turned around in time to get him in the back."

"I'd do the same," Sid said. "But only in Germany."

"Look at what they've done to the Jews," Pete said. (We didn't know the half of it then.)

"I don't believe all that crap about what the Germans have done to the Jews," Henderson, a new pilot, said. "They had it coming to them anyway."

Oh, oh, I thought. But you couldn't head off a jerk like Henderson. I tried, anyway.

"Where are you going on leave next time?" I asked Jim.

But Henderson cut in, "I'm going to London. Never change. But it's getting tougher all the time with those rich Yanks. They must all be Jews."

Oh, well, you asked for it, I thought. Nearly everybody else was studying his heap of butts. I looked at Sid. He lit another cigarette.

"The Temple bar was packed with 'em," Henderson went on. "Those Jews sure get the women, though. I can't understand it. I don't know how those women go out with them."

Sid reached into his tunic pocket and took out a small notebook.

Henderson was babbling on: "Women in Toronto don't go out with the Yids, unless they're Yids themselves."

Jack bent down and pretended to tie a shoelace. George studied his fingernails.

"I'm a Jew," said Sid.

Henderson stopped, and flushed. He fumbled with his tongue. At last he said, "I didn't mean like you. You're different."

Sid put a tick in his notebook.

"See that notebook?" I said to Henderson. "There are two columns in it. One is for the number of guys who say 'but you're different.' The other is for the guys who say 'some of my best friends are Jews.'"

The last time Sid had shown me the book, the two columns were about even, seventy-three ticks on one side, seventy on the other. He had run up this high score by sitting in messes, waiting for the conversation to get around to Jews, then dropping his bomb.

"I have to go to the can," said Henderson.

He left. The can was in another building, without any lights. You had to use a flashlight to find the chemical crapper and the paper, if there was any, which there usually wasn't.

Jack said, "Did you ever put in a third column after what I said?"

"No," said Sid. "I don't get enough of those."

"What did you say?" asked George.

"I'd known Sid for nearly a year before I dropped my brick," Jack said. "D'you know what I said? I said, 'But you don't look like a Jew, Sid'."

That's why Sid had looked so pleased with himself a couple of Sundays ago. The padre was a nice guy and the CO was determined to do something about our not attending his services. He herded a bunch of us into the flight truck and started for the field, where the padre was going to hold forth in a workshop Nissen hut. Sid was coming out of the mess on his way to the ops room. Jack hailed him: "Want a lift, Sid? We're going to church." Sid called back: "No thanks, but you guys go ahead. Some of my best friends are Protestants."

Sid and I discussed religion only once. It was a brief discussion. Sid said, "How arrogant can Christians get? They say man was born in the image of God. Look at what this mage is doing in this war." That seemed to say it all so I didn't say anything.

Sid looked at Jack and grinned. "Now let's talk about frogs," he said.

We all looked at Jobin, the only French-speaking Canadian flier on the squadron. "Perhaps we should wait for Henderson to come back," Jobin said. "I'm not sure he had finished on his subject."

He spoke perfect English. He wanted to be a bomber pilot in No. 6 Group's Alouette squadron. Nobody had the heart to repeat to him what somebody had heard in the Crackers Club: the Alouettes were having a tough time keeping up French-speaking replacements. He would have yearned all the more.

Jobin and I talked now and then about Quebec — in English, of course. I told him I didn't speak French because the dumb Quebec government kowtowed to English-Canadian and American businessmen and didn't enact legislation to make French compulsory in the elementary grades. I didn't see any point to apologizing for not speaking French when it was really all the fault of the French themselves.

This didn't fool Jobin, but he thought it was pretty clever, as I did.

I tried to patronize him in a couple of ways. I said Quebec in 1939 was right to oppose Canada getting into the war. What in hell did Canada have to do with starting the war? But there was Ontario again, ready, aye, ready.

Jobin said we all should have known from what had happened in Spain what was going to happen in 1939. He had been in Spain, it turned out. And had joined the RAF in 1939 and had flown in the Battle of Britain. That set me back a bit.

I also tried out some of my Ontario stories on Jobin. For instance, the one about the Toronto florist who hadn't known the name of his neighbor for eighteen years, until somebody came into the shop one day and ordered a funeral wreath for the address next door. "We had a neighbor like that in Montreal," Jobin said.

The talk came around to zombies. I said there were as many from Saskatchewan as Quebec. Jobin said he doubted it. Zombies were the conscripts in Canada who refused to serve overseas. Once in a while, one of our braves would say that if he had his way, he'd have all the zombies strung up, but most of us were too busily engaged in surviving ourselves to worry about how somebody else was going to prevent himself from being shipped to Europe.

I think we believed in what we were doing, though, without needing to be shown pictures of Belgian babies on the ends of Boche bayonets. The Nazis really were a bunch of bastards. Churchill and everybody else said so. That was good enough for us.

For our squadron, the war was immediate but still far away. There was no other Canadian squadron doing the same work. In the Chez Moi we were often left to talk among ourselves, just as if we were in our own mess. Nobody else had notes to compare with ours.

We were in almost total isolation from the big war. It was as though we were fighting some Arctic Ruritania from an ice floe in the Beaufort Sea. All we knew about was our little war, our twenty-four crews, our little planes, our little thoughts. We didn't know what was going on anywhere else — even in the RAF squadron which occupied the field with us — and we didn't really care.

The one thing we were sure about, and consequently never talked about, was that we were Canadians. It had nothing to do with the war, or patriotism, or the British, or the Americans. It was simply that we were apart. We really were different. We could belong to only one place.

And we had Sid, an American, to confirm it for us. "Why you bastards," he'd say, "you're not American at all."

One afternoon Sid and I flew to Eye, an American air

base in East Anglia, to see Dan, Sid's brother, a Fortress pilot in the U.S. 8th Air Force. The only part of the visit which interested me was that Dan's squadron had lost eight planes two days before when a Jerry intruder got into the main circuit at Eye at dusk when everyone thought all were safely home. The Jerry didn't shoot down eight Fortresses. Four had taken such violent evasive action they had gone into the deck. The Fort squadron had a party the night we were there with a stripper and scotch, but replacements hadn't arrived yet and eighty-eight dead guys left a big, silent gap.

"When do we go?" Sid asked.

I had been daydreaming again about a good pinpoint on the Moselle. And we weren't even going that way. "Not till about half past eleven," I replied.

"I'll get the truck and go get some more cigarettes."

"I'll go over the flight plan again," I said.

"That would be nice. Take out that track over Wiesbaden." The guys around the stove laughed — boy, he was never going to let me forget that one.

Sid was back in a few minutes. "We're scrubbed," he said.

Oh, joy. The greatest word in the language. Scrubbed. Cancelled. Washed out. "Duff weather?"

"Control didn't say." Of course. They never gave a reason. But who cared? We didn't have to go. Reprieve. It was just happiness for the moment. I didn't consider that I had to do thirty-five trips and this cancelled one would have to be replaced some time or other. It was enough I didn't have to go now.

"Is the truck still here?" I asked.

"Yes."

I gathered up my maps and put them in the locker. Boy, could I move quickly now.

"Truck for the Turkey Cock," I shouted, waltzing toward the door. The Turkey Cock was our one village pub. Two other scrubbees joined me, laughing. Sid said he was going to the mess. There might be a scotch there. There wouldn't be any in the pub.

We grabbed the driver at the control tower, frog-marched her to the truck and piled in. Behind the tower. Past the guardhouse. A few bends in the road and there we were.

The door was partly open and three or four locals were standing around outside. "Mind the blackout," shouted the publican from inside. We could barely hear him because of the din inside.

"Can't even get into our own pub," one of the locals grumbled.

"I had to wait half an hour just to get a glass," another said.

"Buy bottled beer instead of the draught," I said.

My two mates and I pushed into the bulging pub. We bucked our way toward the bar. The place was full of ground crew, men and women, and a smattering of locals who had given up trying to look detached from it all.

"Brown ale coming up, Mac." It was Hal, located strategically at the bar. He had ordered a brown ale for me as soon as he had seen me enter. What a ground crew.

I pushed by this little blonde WAAF. It was delightful. I pretended I couldn't get by and remained leaning against her. I was bold in a crowd.

She turned and said: "Leave a little for the next guy."

I pushed on, letting my arm trail behind me so my hand could brush slowly across her behind. What a *boulevardier*.

I grabbed the brown ale from Hal and downed it. "Mrs. Martin," I said to the harassed publican's wife, "a round for my merry men." Boy, was I lightheaded when I got scrubbed.

I fished out some pound notes and put them on the sopping wet bar. She pulled some draughts into used glasses and got some bottled beer from a shelf behind her and took some of the drenched money.

"Boy, that was some trip." Hal was talking about a recent trip where we had hit a train and a couple of truck convoys.

"So-so," I said grandly. Hal thought any trip was great when we came back showing we had fired our guns. Sid had told me he had heard Hal telling another ground crew: "Our boys shoot all the goddam time."

Hal and I took the beers and worked our way over to a table where four guys and two girls were sitting. People kept bumping into me and I slopped draught beer all over the floor and myself. Vallée gave me a light punch in the stomach.

"Watch it," I said, "I'm an air force officer."

Vallée introduced the British girls. "This one really goes for you," Vallée said, indicating the one named Joan. I knew he was lying but I blushed anyway.

Corporal Batten was older than the others. He was also more oiled. He cut right in. "Hey, did you hear this one? A guy comes to a door selling blueberries. This woman answers the door in a negligee. She tells the guy to go around to the back. When he gets there, she's naked. He starts to cry. 'What are you crying for?' she asks. He says, 'On Monday my house burned down. On Tuesday my wife left me. On Wednesday I was fired and on Thursday I lost everything I had left in a poker game. Now you want to fuck me out of my blueberries.'" Batten shouted with laughter and banged the sodden table.

I tried to pretend I hadn't heard him say "fuck" in front of two girls but I blushed anyway. "Look, he's blushing again," Vallée said. A lot of good it did me to be an officer.

"What do you hear from home?" I asked Hal.

"Oh, a good crop," he said, "but no money. All during the thirties we got dried out and hailed out and anything we did grow we got nothing for. Now we have a good crop and a good market. But what do they do? Appeal to the farmer's patriotism to keep the price down. While the manufacturers in the east stick it to everybody in sight, including the farmer as usual."

This carried all of us away on the subject of home. Rich said he was glad he got a chance to get away and would never go back. He came from a farm in Manitoba. But all the rest of us wanted to go home some day.

I felt a bit sorry for the guys who were married and hadn't seen their wives for years. Rich said he had found an easy solution: when he left for overseas, he and his wife agreed that they would both sleep with anybody else any time they felt like it and that when he came home the subject would never be raised by either of them.

"What if she's pregnant or has a kid when you get back?" asked Batten.

"That's part of the agreement. She keeps the kid and if I want I can bring any kids home with me."

He looked at Anne, the other girl at the table. "Don't look at me," she said. The two girls had been totally ignored during the conversation about home. They didn't seem to mind.

Vallée and I went for another load of beer. It was so crowded it took us nearly fifteen minutes. The din reminded me of the British officer describing the 1940 disaster at Dunkirk: "The noise . . . and the people."

Batten was back on everybody's favorite subject. "D'you know the definition of a perfect wife? An over-sexed deaf-mute who owns a liquor store." He began to sing:

Ops in a Mozzie, ops in a Mozzie,
Who'll come on ops in a Mozzie with me?
And he played with his stick as he steered around the
*   Messerschmitt,*
I like to stand up to see Germany.

We were all getting tight by this time. "It's time for 'Alouette'," said O'Brien.

Vallée was on his feet in a flash. Twenty times through it without a stumble. Even a few of the locals looked on appreciatively. It was tough on anybody trying to talk.

Then we were singing "Red River Valley," and "Strawberry Roan," "Lamplighting Time in the Valley," and

"When the Work's All Done This Fall," all the songs we had learned from the *Family Herald* and *Weekly Star*. There were still a lot of farm and village boys then. My cousins could play the fiddle and accordion and sometimes my Aunt Annie jigged on the farmhouse verandah as we soared through our repertoire of a summer's evening.

"Ops in a Wimpy," began Batten, but he was shouted down. He wanted to go through every aircraft in the air force. (The Wimpy was the Wellington bomber.)

We all went for more beer, leaving Batten in charge of the table so none of the locals or anybody else would try to sit down. Mrs. Martin was red in the face. The barmaid with her was drenched. Mr. Martin stood leaning against the bar, talking with another local and no doubt ringing up the take in his head. He never talked with us. He knew whom his customers were going to be when the war ended.

I sat down beside Joan. "Are you with any of these guys?" I asked.

"No," she said. I pulled my chair closer.

"Time, gentlemen, please."

I never could get over how all the publicans called us gentlemen. We paid no attention, of course, until we saw Mrs. Martin having a smoke, the beer handles finally still.

I stole two of Batten's beers when he was looking the other way. "Let's go," I said.

I steered her through the drunks and out the crowded doorway. It was raining. We stumbled along the dark road for a way until we found a telephone box and went in. Wouldn't you know? Some son of a bitch came along and wanted to use it.

We left and found some shelter under the eaves of a building. We felt our way around until we came to a doorway. I was pushing her up against the door when, miraculously, it opened. It was as black as pitch.

"Where in hell are we?"

"It's the gym," Joan said.

We stumbled around and I tripped over something. I got

down on my knees and felt it. "I think it's a wrestling mat," I said. She giggled. "That's appropriate," she said and got down beside me. Before I could experience my usual premature ejaculation, the lights suddenly snapped on.

"Oh, sorry." It was the duty corporal on his rounds. He snapped them off again quickly, but before he did I could make out five other couples on wrestling mats all around the room.

A day or two later, Sid told me he had to go away for five days.

"Where?"

"Alton. I think I've got the clap." Alton was the VD hospital for Canadians. It was located near the Canadian army base at Aldershot, which supplied most of the patients. "Who?" I asked.

"I don't know. It must have been that tiger I met in the Sussex when we were in London a few nights ago." He paused, then added accusingly, "You took me there."

"You went for a scotch, not the clap," I said.

"Well, maybe I haven't got it. The doc says I haven't, that it's just strain. He said if it would make me feel any better he'd send me down to Alton for what they call a test-of-cure. That's what the guys get before they leave, an FFI test."

I didn't wish Sid any bad luck, of course. But five days off were five days out of a Mosquito.

"Are you going to fly with anyone else?" he asked.

"Are you kidding? I wouldn't swap you for Rita Hayworth."

"Well, if you want, take a trip with somebody else," Sid said.

"Are you trying to ditch me?" I asked. There was a new hotshot navigator around with two tours whose pilot had been posted to Canada to give some special instruction at Greenwood, Nova Scotia, an operational training unit. Maybe Sid was thinking that this guy might be able to lead him to where he could shoot down some planes.

Sid grinned. "Hell, no," he said. "You can't navigate worth a damn but you're good company. You keep your mouth shut in the air."

He was back in two days, just as I was getting the feel of lounging around with a glass in my hand, fearless.

"I thought you said you were going to be gone for five days," I said.

"I didn't have it," Sid said. "Of course I knew I didn't but I just wanted to satisfy our doc."

"What happened?"

"The first thing is, I have to go through this army ward. You have to go through it to get to the VD ward. But those army guys aren't there for VD. They're there because they got bombed by our own Lancs in Normandy. Are they cheesed off at the air force. They started throwing things at me, boots, books, anything they could get their hands on. I got the hell out of there as fast as I could.

"There are about twenty-five guys in the VD ward, two rows of beds, most of the guys lying on the beds looking glum, except for the ones expecting to leave in a day or two. One of these guys tells me about this padre who came in as a patient a couple of weeks ago. The padre announces, 'I got it off a bathroom seat' and then he says, 'Here it is' and whips this toilet seat from behind his back and holds it over his head.

"Some of those guys had been there for weeks and weeks. That's what scared me. Penicillin usually gets the clap, but not always. Not the deep-seated stuff, as they call it.

"But what was even more scary was this orderly who came around every morning for a smear. We'd all hold our cocks and he'd take a smear off the end with a little square piece of glass. Then he'd put the glass on his outstretched left arm. He kept all those pieces of glass in a row on his arm, one for each of us, in the same order the beds were in. But once in a while he'd pause and you could just see him thinking: 'Have I got all these in the right order?'

"I figured that if I didn't have the clap, he was going to

give it to me from one of his goddam slides.

"Well, I finally get in for the test. There I am flat on my back and they drop a hockey stick right down my cock. No kidding, this instrument was shaped just like a little hockey stick. The doc peered inside, with all those nurses standing around, and said I looked clean. Later on, they told me I could go next morning. I got up at 5 A.M. and got away before that goddam orderly could come around, and before those soldiers were awake enough to throw anything at me."

I told Sid his talk should replace the chancre movie.

"It's time for an NFT," Sid said, and we went back to flying.

CHAPTER SEVEN

I was going over my flight-plan for the umpteenth time — we were not due off until after midnight — when the call came in from the tower. The weather was so bad over the Continent that only two crews were still on duty and Sid and the other crew were over at the weather office. So I picked up the phone.

"Operations."

"Tower. Three-three's in trouble. One engine. Just thought I'd let you know. Doesn't seem too bad."

"OK. Thanks." I didn't have to look at the board on the wall to know that the crew coming in on one engine was Jobin and Smith. We all recognized each other's call signs.

Jobin had come in on one engine before — twice, in fact. One-engine landings were pretty routine. You had to be damn careful, just the same. There was no going around again if you missed the landing on the first swipe at it.

I went back to my map, trying to find a better pinpoint on the Moselle River. I had difficulty finding any place at night and with the cloud down near the deck it would be hopeless tonight anyway. I finally picked out a bend that I thought might show up, drew a heavy line to it from the previous pinpoint and was just figuring out the new time, distance, and course when I heard the crash truck and meat wagon warming up. Standard procedure. Get them in position to move quickly if there was any trouble. But when the siren went off, I grabbed my hat and ran outside, forgetting to shut the door and letting the light from the naked bulb over the plotting table stream outside. I was running toward the tarmac but I couldn't see the west end of the field because the aircraft bay, ten feet high, nearest the operations hut, blocked my view. I had just turned the corner of the bay when the tower snapped on the floodlights. I stopped. There was three-three burning. I'd seen planes burning before, but never on the ground. There was some shouting behind me and the flight truck started up.

"Over here," Sid yelled.

I ran over to the truck. It was underway before I could pull my right leg in over the tailboard. Sid grabbed my tunic by the shoulder and yanked me inside. I bumped my shin on the wooden bench running down the right side of the truck.

"What happened?"

"Overshoot," Jack said. "We were just coming out of weather and he went by like a bat out of hell. Pulled the undercart up, I guess. Bellied in."

"Maybe he forgot to switch off the gas," George said. Sid looked at me. He, like I, was thinking of High Ercall.

The flight commander was sitting up front with the driver. Sid, Jack, George, and I sat back under the canvas. We were racing down the perimeter track. Two more fire trucks screamed across the field. It was as bright as day under the floodlights.

"Fine blackout," said Jack in an attempt to be light. Nobody responded.

We were there in a minute. I didn't want to get out of the truck. Sid jumped down, ran around the back and then toward the burning aircraft. Jack and George ran, too. I got down after a while and forced myself to look. There was nothing any of us could do.

The plane had swerved around 180 degrees and we were looking directly at the nose as the floodlights poured into the cockpit. The fire trucks got out their hoses as fast as they could and sprayed the plane. But the wooden wonder burned too quickly, too fiercely. I could see Jobin and Smith struggling. It was no use — they were trapped. Nobody could get close with the flames and the heat and they couldn't get out of the cockpit. The crash had jammed the door and the only way they could get out was through the perspex roof. It was jammed too.

I couldn't move. I wanted to go back behind the truck so that I couldn't see what was going on but I couldn't move. I couldn't even shut my eyes. Jobin struck at the top hatch. He hit it again and again with his bare fist. His wrist twisted over suddenly and he began hitting the hatch with his other hand. Smith didn't seem to move at all, but his mouth was opening and closing. I could almost look down his throat. I couldn't stand any more. Jobin and Smith were roasting right in front of us. Their clothes started to smoulder and then they caught fire. Jobin's helmet had come off and his hair was blazing. Somebody screamed "Luc, Luc," and ran toward the fire but somebody else jumped and tackled him and others rushed up to hold him.

Their faces became redder and redder. And over the sounds of the flames and the hoses, the sirens and the helpless shouts came the screams from inside the plane. I guess none of us could look away. The floodlights fixed the cockpit with a steady, gigantic eye. Jobin's and Smith's mouths were wide open and their faces started to turn black before the screaming stopped. I didn't move, even when the port wing tank exploded and the ammo started to pop off.

I vomited. I didn't even lower my head or bend over. I just opened my mouth and the vomit ran down my chin and over my tunic, yellow over blue. I could hear sobbing but I didn't know whether it was Luc's friend or somebody else. I felt somebody grip my arm.

"Come on, let's go." It was Sid. But I couldn't move. I didn't retch. The vomit just ran out of my throat and mouth and down my chest. Sid came around in front of me, grabbed me by the shoulders and shook me as hard as he could.

"Let's go," he repeated.

We walked back to the truck. The driver wasn't there and the flight commander got behind the wheel. We went back to the ops room. I wasn't the only one who had been sick. Sid and I sat down by the stove and Sid shook out his cigarettes. I looked into the open door of the stove where some wet wood and coal were smouldering. Sid lit a cigarette and gave it to me. We just sat there for a long time looking at the smoking coal in the stove.

"Your flight plan finished?"

"No," I said.

He got up and walked into the cubbyhole where the board and the telephone were. I could hear Sid talking with control. He came back to the stove and said, "Let's go home. We're scrubbed." I knew we hadn't been cancelled. We were on standby for the next two hours. But I didn't protest or say I was fine or anything like that.

Mary was in the flight truck waiting and we drove down to the house. I sat in the back because I stank so much.

It was about a ten-minute drive. We got out and started up the four steps to the entrance. Sid said, "Wait a minute." He pulled off my tunic and threw it in the grass. "Wipe your face off," he said. I pulled out my handkerchief and wiped my face and threw the handkerchief near the jacket. We went up the narrow stairs and undressed in the dark so that we wouldn't have to fix the blackout. We got into our cots. I went to sleep right away. I never had any trouble sleeping while I was on the squadron, except the odd time, even after that fire. It was only after I left the squadron I couldn't sleep, even with a lot of booze in me.

I was cold when I woke up, but that didn't mean anything. I was cold all the time I was in England. I heaped on the blankets but they were always sodden with the damp. The blankets became so heavy I had to lie on my side to keep their weight off my chest. It was foggy, I was glad to see. But then I remembered we weren't on that day, anyway.

Sid was already dressed. "Did you sleep?" he asked.

"I always think I'll never be able to sleep and then I drop off like a baby," I said. "How about you?"

"OK," he said.

Sid sometimes had nightmares. He would shout in his sleep and wake me up. And once or twice he walked in his sleep. One night in that grubby little room I woke up and Sid was standing beside his cot waving his arms and shouting "searchlights" over and over again. It struck me that if I were to shout in my sleep like that it would be "flak, flak," but it was one of those odd things that flak didn't bother Sid much, but searchlights did. He just didn't like sitting up there in a light so blinding you couldn't read your instrument panel. I didn't like searchlights either but compared with flak aimed straight at your balls through a wooden plane they were fairly benign.

"Where's my tunic?" I asked.

"Outside. You puked all over it."

I didn't say anything to that. When I got my shirt on, I put my leather jacket on over it and went outside. I rolled the tunic in a towel to take up to the mess. I put the handkerchief under a rock.

It was almost noon. Sid came down the rickety little staircase and we stood in the unpainted hall, waiting for the truck. The house had belonged to some wealthy family at one time but it was falling apart now. There was no water. The garden was overgrown and the little creek at the back was clogged with refuse. Jack came out of his front room and joined us.

"Where did you get to last night?" Sid asked Jack.

"The CO gave me a lift to the mess and we had a few drinks. But nobody felt much like drinking and I walked back."

"You walked?" Nobody ever walked unless the pub stayed open late or the crews were all down and Mary had gone to bed.

A horn blew. We went outside into the gravel road (it ended at the house and the creek). Sid and I got in the front seat with Mary, who had red hair and a tiny waist. The others straggled out of the house one by one and got into the back. We had to wait five minutes for Bill. He came out doing up his fly. Nobody paid any attention to Mary. But we all liked her. The first two ready always sat with her in the front.

We took the winding road to the mess, past the south side of the field and the dripping swamp. We couldn't see the wreck. Mary didn't volunteer any information. She just drove a bunch of guys from the house to the mess to the flight and back again and all of a sudden some of them didn't get in the truck any more.

The truck ran up the lane beside the lawn and under the oak trees to the white house where the rest of the crews lived. I ran into the padre on the way to the bar. I tried not to notice him, thinking he was going to ask me to go on the funeral detail, though that wasn't up to him. His request was even worse. He wanted me to write to Smith's relatives. The word always got around that I had written sports for the *Varsity* (I advertised it) and this made me fair game for letter writing.

"Did you know Smith well?" the padre asked.

"Not well," I said. "Jack knew him a lot better." I looked around but neither Jack nor Sid was anywhere in sight.

"I was wondering whether you'd write Smith's wife," he said.

"Doesn't the CO or the padre do that?" I asked, trying to be pleasant at the same time, but failing, as usual.

"Yes, we do. But something from you chaps is better. Closer to home, as it were."

"I'll try in the next day or two," I said. Then I forgot about it. What in hell could I say to Smith's wife?

I looked at the notice board. Thank God I wasn't on the funeral party. They probably thought I'd puke again.

We weren't a big enough squadron to have both a Protestant and a Catholic padre. So a Catholic priest was imported from another field for Jobin. The black remains were divided into two boxes and buried under the pine trees on the far side of the field.

Trip No. 26 was to Jagel and Husum in southern Denmark. We always called them trips or ops. We never used the American "mission," thinking it slightly evangelical. It was a long way to Denmark, but all of it over the sea, thank heaven.

Hal wasn't in the dispersal when we took off and then I remembered we had B Baker and not P Peter. Our own plane was in for a major engine overhaul.

We presumed the bombers might be having a go at Kiel because Jagel was about fifteen miles northwest of Kiel. Husum was on Denmark's west coast and due west of Jagel. But when we got in the area there was no activity at all. There were no fires in, or searchlights from, Kiel, and both Jagel and Husum were as quiet as church mice.

That suited me fine. We circled one field, then went over to circle the other, waiting for somebody to turn on their lights. Suddenly, my ears pricked up at a funny noise. The starboard engine had started to act up.

"Give me a course home," Sid said.

It was simple, just the reverse of the trip out. Course 080 degrees out meant 260 degrees back. "Two-six-zero," I said. We were out over the coast quickly. It would be an hour back to England over the North Sea.

The engine was running roughly. "I'm going to feather," Sid said.

He got some more height and then pushed the big button which stopped the engine and propellor on my side. The speed dropped from 240 to 180. This was going to add at least fifteen minutes to the trip home.

"I'm getting tired of going home on one engine," I said.

"No wonder, you have nothing to keep you occupied," said Sid.

I didn't even have to look out the back because it was ten-tenths cloud. Sid had to keep his eyes on his instruments without a break.

"Let's hope that port engine holds up," Sid said. "This is what happens when we don't have our own plane."

I kept looking in the direction of the port engine, hoping to encourage it. We droned on. Nothing needed to be said, so nothing was said. I calculated that we were about fifteen minutes from Coltishall on the English coast when the port engine suddenly went. A lick of flame showed over the cowling. First I froze. Then I began shaking.

"Get out," Sid said. He might just as well have told me to recite the Old Testament. I couldn't move.

"Get out," he repeated. His voice was a little harsher.

My mouth was open and I could taste the sloe gin dribbling out of the corners. God, I had to do something.

There was another lick of flame from the port engine this time a little bigger and longer. I felt for my dinghy hitches. That was something. I had remembered to fasten the dinghy to my parachute harness. Next, the parachute. It was on the floor between my feet. I leaned over to pick it up but my straps were too tight and I couldn't reach it. I tried again but my fingers just brushed the chute.

"Get out," Sid said a third time.

I hit the release on the second attempt and got my straps off.

I thought, I don't know how to bail out. Even if I get down I'll never get into the dinghy. Even if I get into the dinghy nobody will ever find me. I'll just blow my whistle and blow and blow and nobody will ever hear it. We carried a whistle fastened to the neck of the tunic but the only time I had ever used it was to try to attract the attention of Mr. Martin in the Turkey Cock.

I got over far enough this time to reach the parachute. But my hands were trembling so badly I couldn't pick it up. I thought I had a grip on it but then I would lose it.

"You yellow bastard," Sid shouted.

With my fingers and legs, I worked the chute up to between my knees. I got it around the right way so that it would hook onto the harness on my chest. But the fasteners were stiff and I was still shaking and I dropped it again. I'd end up pulling the handle and the chute would unfold in the cockpit.

"You bastard, I'm going to get this thing back," Sid said. "Now listen, I'm going to restart that starboard engine. As soon as I give the word, you shove the fire extinguisher for the port engine. And make goddam sure it's the port."

He pushed the starboard restart button. The prop began to turn and the engine caught. Sid waited a few seconds, then said, "Now."

I pushed the extinguisher button and the flames died out with a final spurt. The starboard engine was rough but it was going.

The manual said you could survive only half an hour in the North Sea if you didn't get into a dinghy. The body quickly contracted from the cold, like glue drying.

Sid switched on the transmitter. "Mayday, Mayday, Mayday," he said. We were telling England we needed help. I watched the starboard prop like a hawk.

"Mayday, Mayday, Mayday," Sid repeated after a minute.

Some seconds went by and then I could hear, "Windsock. Steer two-five-five." Windsock was Coltishall.

"About nine minutes, I think," I said.

"Oh, you're still there," Sid said. "I thought you bailed out."

I could take any number of remarks like that if he could get me back.

"Credo two-nine," Sid said into the transmitter. "Single engine. How far?"

"Windsock. Two-five-six. Seven minutes. Do you need anything?"

"Credo two-nine. Luck. Thank you."

"Windsock. Fog here. Come straight in."

I was straining my eyes ahead for some sight of Coltishall. At least my eyes worked, if my hands didn't. Sid sat hunched over, coaxing the starboard engine with the throttle.

The cloud gave out as we neared the coast. But it was replaced by fog, which seemed to be thickening. Sid began to take us down.

"Credo two-nine, this is Windsock. Steer five degrees starboard. You are approaching the perimeter."

We couldn't see damn all.

"Final approach," said Windsock.

Suddenly, I could make out a dim flarepath through the fog. "There it is," I yelled.

"I've got it," Sid said. He stuck the nose down and we landed more than halfway down the runway. Coltishall was longer than our own field and we had room to slow down.

Sid pulled off the runway and stopped. "Another fifteen minutes and we wouldn't have seen anything," Sid said.

"Credo two-nine. Very nice. We'll get you."

In a minute a jeep arrived and we followed it through the gathering fog to a dispersal. By the time we got there we could hardly make out the blue and amber taxiing lights.

"Christ, you're good at this," I said just before the door opened.

"Yeah? I noticed you still cling to that windowledge during my landings."

I went down to the field for a night flying test and I saw Sid talking with Russ Bannock in a corner of the ops room. Sid came over to me a minute later, all smiles, and announced: "We're going to Denmark again."

I didn't receive news of any trip with joy. I was even less enthusiastic about Denmark.

"In daylight," Sid said.

"Jesus," I whispered. I knew this had to come sooner or later: a daylight ranger. It was on these daylight operations that the squadron had scored most of its kills.

"Russ thinks we're ready," Sid said.

"Ready?" I squeaked. I knew Sid had been badgering Russ for weeks to go on a day ranger. That was all the permission needed. Fighter Command had given the squadron a free hand to roam all over hell's half-acre in Europe in daylight if it wanted. And to these crazy pilots there was nothing better.

The official history of the RCAF Overseas, Vol. III, page 317, describes Sid as "an American Jewish boy who wanted to get into the business of hammering Hitler." It really says that, on page 317.

"You won't have to navigate," Sid said.

"What?"

"We're going with Russ, and Bob will do the navigation. Of course, you'll have to keep track and take over if anything happens to Russ." Bob Bruce was Russ's navigator, a calm, cool, pipe-smoking Welshman who studied music. "You look out the back, that's all you have to do," said Sid. Five to six hours of pretzeldom.

Sid was hopping around in sheer delight. Up to this point, all we'd seen in the way of an enemy aircraft was the odd stab of light which might or might not have been a plane. We'd done twenty-seven trips and Sid was beginning to feel he'd get through a whole tour without ever seeing an enemy plane, let alone get a shot at one.

I thought he was going to whirl around the room, his finger pointing, yelling "rat-à-tat-tat-rat-a-tat-tat," or "bang, bang, you're dead."

"When do we go?" I asked.

"Well, it's too late today," Sid said, "so we'll try for tomorrow morning."

"What's the target?"

"Some place called Vaerlose. Bob knows where it is.'

"Is that the only place?"

"I think so."

That was a relief. Bannock usually liked a nice selection of several targets. But he could easily decide at Vaerlose to call in at airfields near Berlin on the way home. I don't think he had any nerves. But he didn't push this at any of us. I think he was perfectly willing to accept that some of us were scared to death and he did not attach any blame to it. He never raised his voice. He never swore.

We were going straight into Vaerlose and straight out. Takeoff 0835, depending on weather. The perfect weather for a ranger was a lot of cloud, so that you pull up into it if you were chased by a fighter. We would travel right on the deck just high enough to clear the trees and buildings. More than one of our guys had been chased on the deck by fighters, been damaged but made it home. We figured that if there was no cloud cover and we saw the fighter first so that we had time to get up to full throttle before he came at us, we had a fair chance of getting away on the deck. This was because the fighter had a difficult time flying right on the deck and shooting at the same time. If he got too interested in the gunsight, he might plough right into the deck. Conversely, if he was paying strict attention to his height, he couldn't concentrate on his shooting. Jas and Archie had been chased by an FW-190 and had lived to tell about it. They had had part of their tail shot away but they had fled over the sea and the fighter had given up.

Bob was puffing on his pipe and drawing up a flight plan. I don't know which he took more seriously. He showed me the route on his map and I copied all his work onto mine. Vaerlose was twelve miles northwest of Copenhagen, beautiful, beautiful Copenhagen.

No drinks that night. I slept OK, as usual, but I couldn't eat any breakfast. All I could get down was a bit of powdered milk.

We met Russ and Bob at the ops room. "How's the weather?" I asked, still hoping against hope that we might be scrubbed.

"Great," said Russ.

I don't think he or Sid gave a damn whether there was a patch of cloud cover. Bob just shrugged. He was used to this.

I had a bit of a problem having my superstitious pee under the port wing of the Mosquito because it was broad daylight. I had to wait for Mary to leave with the truck, with Sid muttering impatiently and Russ and Bob peering over curiously from their bay. But I managed near the port wheel.

We took off behind Russ and I looked down, as I did on each afternoon we did a night flying test, at the burned-out patch in the grove where Macdonald and Jones had died. They had pulled up too quickly and the plane had fallen over on its side, like a bird shot in the wing. Straight down it had gone, just a little way, leaving a puff of fire, a puff of smoke, the green oak shrivelling black. In the morning light, the sun struck a piece of still shiny metal.

Out over East Anglia we went, heading for Coltishall from where we would set course. The great bomber bases were quiet now except for the ground crews preparing the Lancs and Hallies for their night's work. Bottisham and Snailwell, Castle Camps and Stradishall, Bury St. Edmunds and Snetterton Heath, Bungay and Horsham St. Faith, Coningsby and Fiskerton, Carfoss and Hutton Cranswick, all Butcher Harris's sources of manpower. I had bunked with some of the bomber boys when I had been training at Cranwell. We slept on the dining-room floors in the overcrowded hotels of Lincoln. I went back to my radio course. They went back in the chill morning buses to their bomber bases and the mass briefings on the target for the night.

We were soon over the North Sea, in the same area where Sid had asked me to leave the plane. A calm ocean, a sunny day, the two Mosquitoes low over the water, Sid astern and to starboard of Russ in No. 2 position. Ordinarily, that

would gall Sid, but we were on our way in daylight and th
was all that mattered to him for the moment.

We had to stay low to keep under their radar. Jer
wouldn't have a clue where we were until we arrived
Denmark, and then he couldn't tell very well which directic
we were going. I hoped.

"Look out the back," Sid said. I surveyed an empt
glittering sky.

"Where's the cloud cover?" I asked.

"Up ahead, I guess," Sid said.

I could read weather as well as he could and I knew ther
wouldn't be a cloud bigger than a man's hand the whole da

Bob had planned to hit the Danish coast just after w
passed the north end of the island of Romo. That's exactl
where we arrived.

"Some navigation," Sid said, glancing across at me.

"Watch the ground," I snapped, bravely.

There's an easy trick to low-level navigation: Kno
where you start and then never lose track of your exac
position for a second. If your attention is diverted even fo
only a short span, you can get lost because the railways
roads, rivers, and lakes flash by quickly when you're brushin
the treetops.

Denmark was beautiful. Fall was just coming on. Th
white and red houses were lit by the morning sun.

Despite the instructions to look out the back, I decide
I'd better try my hand at European low-level navigation. I'
better learn fast because I figured this wouldn't be the onl
daylight ranger we'd do — if we got back from this one, o
course.

First minute from the coast: a road, then a railway
Second minute: highway across the Gels river, a grove, th
Flads river, another grove. Third minute: railway and roac
due north and south, a creek, a road, the village of Jels
Fourth minute: a railway, a creek, another railway, bendin
from east to north. Fifth minute: village of Taps and
highway, minor road and railway, a 100-foot hill we went u

and over, water. We were already across the narrow waist of Denmark. This was Little Belt. We were across the strait in another minute, the water as blue as I had ever seen, everything clean and fresh. Where was the war? Seventh minute: over the north end of the island of Fyn, a road, a railway, the village of North Aaby, a highway, the village of Braenderup, a railway junction. Eighth minute: along the railway for thirty seconds, a creek, the village of Sonderse. Ninth minute: a road, a railway, another road, the village of Otterup, supposed to be a flak site just south of it, all quiet. Tenth minute: Odense Fiord, a round-headed peninsula, an inlet, a road, a railway. Russ turned slightly to starboard, we followed. Eleventh minute: water again, the Great Belt, Romso Island to starboard, two and one-quarter minutes over water, sand beach, pretty cottages, where did the Danes find all the paint? We're now over the island of Sjaelland where Copenhagen — and Vaerlose — are located. Thirteenth minute: a creek, a road, a railway and the village of Gorlev, all together, another creek, lake to port, don't see it because we're too low. Fourteenth minute: east-west road, village of Ruds Vedby with railway track, a grove. Fifteenth minute: nothing for a whole minute but open field, crossed by one road. Sixteenth minute: road, road, railway, a sudden ridge which we mount and descend. Seventeenth minute: highway, double railway. Eighteenth minute: railway, road, road, highway, Koge Bay. Nineteenth minute: turn due north after forty-five seconds over water. Twentieth minute: coast again, those beautiful cottages, small boats bobbing at anchor, but nobody in sight, look far to starboard in direction of Kastrup, Copenhagen's main airfield — no planes in air, thank heaven — a highway and secondary field, again nothing in sight. Twenty-first minute: double railway, highway, railway, road, Russ and Sid swinging hard to port. Twenty-second minute: a grove, a pond, Vaerlose.

We had to pull up to be able to see anything on the ground at Vaerlose. There were some planes parked on the far side of the field near the hangars.

Russ, in the lead, began firing first, at the planes to the left. I got a glimpse of an explosion. Sid opened up on the planes parked to the right. My feet began jumping because of the banging of the cannons under the floorboards.

Sid made some strikes on one or two planes. My attention was diverted by a strange sight to starboard. A man in overalls was on the top of a ladder painting the front part of a hangar, the section over the big doors. He was a good twenty feet in the air. He had tried to get down the ladder too quickly when he heard us and had pushed the ladder out from the wall. He teetered at the top of the ladder, his arms flailing like some hilarious clown circus act. The ladder slowly went over and the man fell backwards in a ninety-degree arc. Before he hit the pavement in front of the hangar, we were gone.

"Goddam it," said Sid. "They wouldn't burn."

I looked back and saw what he meant. Russ had hit two planes and both were on fire. Sid had hit two, and nothing had happened except that some pieces had flown off.

A squirt of flak came up just as Sid put the Mosquito into a deep turn. "We'll try again," Sid said.

He was turning so steeply the blood started to drain out of my head. There was a crackle in the earphones. "Don't go back, Sid," Russ said.

God bless you, Russ Bannock, I thought.

Sid mumbled something but he didn't question the order, which had broken the silence since takeoff between our two planes. He pushed the stick the other way and we began to level out and, more important, put distance between us and the field. There were a couple more rounds of flak but apparently it didn't come anywhere near us. As long as i missed, I didn't care how narrow or wide the miss was.

"Goddam it," Sid said.

He was burned up that he had only damaged two planes while Russ had destroyed two. How in hell was he going to whip Hitler single-handedly if he couldn't shoot straight.

than that? I could practically hear the words going through his head.

"Well, at least we saw some Jerries," I said.

It didn't appease him. "What in hell is the point of seeing Jerries if we can't knock them off?"

"Maybe we got a real one," I said.

"What?"

I told him about the guy falling off the ladder.

"Is that what you were watching?" Sid asked.

"It took my mind off the shooting," I said.

"Jesus."

I began to take in the beauty of the Danish countryside again.

"Look out the back," Sid said. As I turned, I looked at the gyro heading. We were steering about 315 degrees instead of the 270 which was the shortest way home.

"Where in hell are we going?" I demanded.

"Do you expect Russ to call us up and announce it to the Jerries?"

But I had already guessed. Aalborg was the biggest German air base in the north of Denmark. Sure enough, out over the Kattegat we sped, our props nearly touching the water. There was a slight ripple on the sea. Sometimes when it was dead calm it was difficult to judge your height and some guys had gone into the drink. But this was more likely to happen over a lake than over an arm of the ocean.

I wasn't as worried as much as I thought I'd be, headed for an unexpected second target. The main reason, I guess, was the knowledge that Russ didn't want to risk having the hell shot out of his men for the sake of having a second pass at a field in daylight. That was the big difference between night and daylight operations. At night, you could hang around a field for an hour or two. You might not be able to see them but by God they couldn't see you. In daylight, you were a target all the time if there was flak anywhere nearby.

It took us fifteen minutes to get to Aalborg. Bob hit the entrance of the Langerak, a long, wide inlet to the Kattegat, cut across the south of the city and then turned due north. The airfield was on the northwest outskirts of the city. We pulled up to look, as we had done at Vaerlose. I couldn't see anything. Russ took the left side of the drome, we took the right. Nothing. Even better, there was no flak. We pulled off to port and in less than two minutes were over the Skagerrak, thence to the North Sea, and homeward bound.

We didn't say anything for half an hour. Then Sid said, "Why don't you do something?"

It was true. He had to do all the work. On legs of a trip which covered a lot of water, there was nothing much the navigator could do. "I prefer to leave everything in your capable hands." I meant it. His hand on the stick was strong and steady. But I should have said nothing.

"Christ, all that way and only two damaged." Sid reflected for a moment. "You have to hit the wing roots. I guess I hit the cockpits." We had been trained that in shooting at a plane on the ground it was best to aim for the spot where the wings join the fuselage. There was a better chance of hitting the fuel tanks.

"Well, you don't have all day to aim in a situation like that," but I couldn't console him. I told him again about the guy going over backwards from the hangar. This brightened him up a bit.

"I wonder if we could claim one German destroyed," he mused.

"If he was a German."

"Of course he was a German," he said. "It's a German base."

"Maybe they hire some Danes as painters."

"Never," he said. He was adamant on the point. It was strange how these individuals we encountered on the ground along our route created little incidents in our trips. They are incidents which I remember far better than cannonading convoys and trains.

We got back to Hunsdon about 1400. Russ came over to our Mosquito after we landed and said, "Nice going, Sid."

"Nice shooting," Sid said. "I didn't shoot so hot."

"Oh, there'll be plenty of trips yet," Russ said. I wished he hadn't said that. It made me start thinking of the next trip before I could enjoy the relief of being back from this one.

We went through the usual debriefing with the intelligence officer. Russ claimed a Junkers 88 and Messerschmitt 110 destroyed. Sid claimed a Focke-Wulf 190 and Messerschmitt 110 damaged.

Sid's spirits picked up that night in the mess.

"Any joy?" The usual question.

"One Jerry destroyed," Sid said.

"Great. Nice going. Knew you'd break the ice."

"You want to hear how?"

"Sure. You bet. Wouldn't miss it."

"Well, we pull up to get a look at this field and there are some fighters parked on the far side. Russ starts shooting and I go in after him. I'm getting ready to hit this FW when this guy on a ladder starts waving to me. Frantically. He's way the hell up on this ladder painting the hangar. And there he is waving, like he knew me all his life. I'm trying to get the hang of what he's trying to tell me and I take my eye off the FW. A couple of pieces fly off the FW but that's all. I was too distracted by this guy. By this time, he's going over backwards and the last we see of him he's head down like a guy off a thirty-foot diving board, and still waving. I get ready to go back to see if he left any last word but Russ wouldn't let me. I told Collie (the intelligence officer) that I was claiming one Jerry destroyed. Next time I hope there are no greeters to distract me."

We went twice more to Copenhagen, both times to inspect Kastrup airfield. Once was a standard night trip, the other a day ranger.

On the night trip, it was clear and we could easily make out the peninsula which hangs down into Koge Bay and on which Kastrup is located.

Just across the sound, in Sweden, the city of Malmo was all lit up. It was the first time we had seen a city lighted by electricity rather than bombs since we had left Canada.

"Tempting, isn't it?" I said to Sid. I had peered at my map and there were three nice airfields in the immediate vicinity of Malmo.

"Naw," Sid said. "Spend the rest of the war with Swedish blondes? Why, the war might go on for years."

I didn't care what he said, it was still tempting. But Sid was the driver. There was no way I could knock him on the head and land at Malmo.

"Engines OK?" I asked.

Sid laughed and pretty soon we started west, the long way to safety.

Halfway across the North Sea, Sid suddenly exclaimed "Christ, I put red on blue."

My heart skipped a beat. This meant he had put the compass on reverse, so that we were flying east instead or west.

"We must be over Finland somewhere," Sid said.

My knees came together convulsively. But for once I used my head. I glanced up and the North Star was on my side, the starboard side, the side it should be on if we were going west.

"Don't kid me," I said, but I couldn't keep the relief out of my voice.

"Had you going that time," Sid said, chortling into his mask. The bastard. As if I didn't have frights enough, without him inventing some additions. Still, he could sure drive a plane.

In the mess: "You should have seen my alligator when I told him we were over Finland and headed for Moscow. He nearly fainted dead away. Then I could see him looking for a pinpoint over Finland, except we don't carry any maps of Finland but he forgot that and was looking on some other map, just looking for some pinpoint. He was pretty good though. He remembered to find the North Star. I don't know what he would've done if we'd been in cloud."

I hated to think of that myself. Rick gave me the old sign

for the twitching rectum and all I could do was shrug agreement.

As for the Copenhagen daylight trip, things went just the way I liked — uneventfully.

We had about three and a half minutes to go before leaving the Danish coast, going home, when we flew over a small pond. There was a man standing up in a flat-bottomed boat fishing. I remember noting that his boat was headed the same way we were.

It's damn scary for anybody if a low-flying plane comes up from behind like that. There's no sound until the last second. But the guy in the boat didn't flinch. He didn't even duck. He hauled a pistol out of a holster on his right hip and began blazing away at us like some western badman.

Sid didn't see the man pull out his sixshooter. I could see such things better because I wasn't flying the machine. "Hey, that guy took a shot at us," I said.

I should have known better.

"Why, the son of a bitch," Sid said and began to pull up. I knew what he was going to do. He was going to circle and blow the son of a bitch right out of the water.

"Keep down," I yelled. "Sylt's coming up." The island of Sylt was heavily defended. It was German territory attached to the German coast by a causeway. It defended the air approaches to Flensburg and Kiel.

"What?" Sid said, but he put the nose down and we continued on our course. We were supposed to come out seven miles north of Sylt.

"We might be a little south of track," I said. Actually, we were dead on course, but I didn't want him fooling around trying to knock off a lone fisherman, while we gave a Jerry fighter a chance to spot us.

"Shall I turn north?" Sid said.

"No, stay on this for a minute." A moment or two later I said, "Oh, I guess we're all right," as we arrived at the coast and flew seaward between two small islands, neither of them Sylt.

"Well you bastard," said Sid.

"Pretty good navigation, eh?"

"You bastard Jerry-lover," he said.

"Just a Christian gentleman," I said.

"A scared Christian gentleman."

"Amen."

We went home and the next day we did some practice attacks on ground targets. Sid hadn't forgotten missing at Vaerlose. He took the camera out of the nose and later we looked at the film.

"A kill every time," Sid pronounced.

CHAPTER EIGHT

I was named to the squadron's top committee: party organization. I didn't understand this high appointment by the two flight commanders until I discovered all the committee members were considered to be lushes.

Our job was to round up drinks for a squadron party to celebrate our destruction of 100 Jerry planes in the air. We could have had the party months earlier but it wasn't good form to include planes destroyed on the ground. After all, there was nobody in them, except perhaps for some poor erk fixing an electrical circuit or something.

We — the committee — hit on the brilliant idea of dispatching a plane to France to pick up some champagne. We had quick volunteers. We collected some money, though we didn't see any reason why the French shouldn't give us champagne free in recognition of our heroic efforts in their liberation. We forgot the army was there a long time ahead of us.

The committee was astute in the collection of funds. Light-fingered Eddie was appointed to get into the squadron strongbox by any available method and put his hands on as many escape kits as he could. The kits contained European currency but we were surprised, when Eddie presented the committee with a dozen, how few francs were in each.

"How in hell could we escape with one of those?" said Pete. "There's not enough money to put up in a hotel for one night."

"You're not supposed to stay in a hotel," Mickey said. "You're supposed to stay with the farmer's daughter."

A subcommittee was formed to visit the local breweries in the hope we would receive donations in return for protecting them from doodlebugs and other terrors of the night. This subcommittee comprised ten men travelling in two Austins. The membership changed frequently to accommodate all the requests. As a result, I made only one visit, but it was one of the most unforgettable visits I ever made.

I was considered, in my own estimation if nobody else's, an expert on brown ale. We trooped off to a brewery in Ware, only ten miles away, which bottled a very nice brown ale.

The manager greeted us like long-lost sons. He was a cheery, red-faced and, oddly enough, thin man in his late fifties. He knew exactly what we were about. He led us to a special room which had a big round table and shelves of bottles behind a bar.

"Perhaps you'd like to start with this one," he said. I liked that word "start."

Ten of us sat around the table, which must have been made for this very purpose, and tried a nice brown ale, pouring it slowly into the glasses the manager provided.

"Perhaps you'd like to make sure by just trying another bottle of the same," he said.

"Yes, I think we should make sure," Jack said.

We finished that and the manager suggested a lighter ale. It proved very smooth.

"Now here's something a little lighter — and perhaps a little stronger," the manager said. "The bathroom's right there behind the bar, room for three at a time."

He tried to pass around some Woodbines but we insisted that he have some of our Canadian cigarettes.

We tried another beer. "It is difficult to decide, isn't it?" he said.

We had to make sure on that one, too.

"Maybe you'd like to go back to the first one."

"Is anybody here flying tonight?" Jack said.

No.

"Well, no reason not to try just another, is there?" the manager said. He produced a form and asked the self-advertised expert in brown ale to sign it.

"Certainly," I said. He gave me a copy and I put it in my tunic.

I fished it out the next day when I was hunting for my cigarettes. One hundred cases of brown ale at £2 a case.

"Jesus," I said to Jack, "I thought they were making a donation."

"They did," Jack said. "To the subcommittee only." He added after a pause: "I see that you signed it."

I asked Sid what I should do. "You know I drink only scotch," he said.

The party was a big success. The CO, who was Russ Bannock by this time, took the bill off my hands and I never heard of it again.

The champagne, in modest amount, arrived from Carpiquet airfield in Normandy. The volunteers were unable to buy from a Frenchman. Some Canadian army bandit held them up for all their money in exchange for a dozen bottles.

The two volunteers landed, took the champagne to the party room, went upstairs for a shower, returned, and all the champagne had been drunk. They didn't get a sip.

"Brown ale is better for your bowels," Sid said, handing each of them a bottle. He was sipping scotch and he had some ice in it. I never found out where he got the ice. There wasn't any in England except in his glass.

Johnson and Gibbons had shot down the 100th Jerry

and they were properly thanked for having provided a sound motive for the party.

But the guy we all crowded around was Rafe who had rejoined the squadron that day. He had been shot down over Belgium months before and nobody had ever expected to see him again. But there he was, expansive as ever, a big man, laughing, one arm cradling several drinks which had been brought to him, the other flourishing the immediate drink and a cigar. He told us the damnedest story we had ever heard. I relate it in condensed form.

"We got out of the plane OK but I landed a long way from Bud and I didn't seen him again. I buried the parachute and walked as far as I could that night. I was tripping over everything in the dark so I found a road and just stuck to it. I saw a farmhouse just before dawn so I got into the barn and into the hay and went to sleep.

"The farmer comes out the next morning and he's not surprised at all to find me. He gets me some food and tells me to sit tight, just wait, do nothing.

"Two nights later another guy comes and the farmer says for me to go with him. The farmer's a member of an escape group, for God's sake.

"This other guy takes me to another house where they give me some civvy clothes and then another guy comes and he takes me to another house. Anyway, I end up in Brussels in this apartment and there's this dame living there. She's in the underground, too.

"Well, we get pretty friendly. In fact, we're in the sack most of the time. Another guy comes one night and he and my girl have a big argument. She keeps saying no, it's not safe.

"One day, she says we're to go together and off we go that night, sneaking around the streets, and into another apartment where there are some old folks she knows. An aunt and uncle, I guess.

"Anyway, we stay there for a few weeks and I'm enjoying everything and she is, too, and this guy comes again and says I have to move on. She says OK and Annette and I that night go to another place on the outskirts of Brussels. I don't really care what's going on because I'm having a good time. But it finally comes to me that Annette and I are running away from the underground instead of the Germans. They want to get me back to England and she wants to keep me there.

"It took them four weeks to find us this time. Three guys come in the middle of the night. One of them grabs her and locks her in a closet and stands in front of the door. The other two guys tell me we're on our way to the next underground stop.

"I got passed along the route through France to Spain and here I am, all tuckered out trying to escape from the escape route."

Rafe went back flying. He went missing on his first trip. Did he ask his navigator to jump, then jump himself in the vicinity of Brussels? Just looking up an old friend, so to speak. We never found out what happened to him. There are so many stories from the war which have no known endings.

In the last half of September and early October, Sid and I were assigned a bunch of rotten airfields to cover. The weather was bad, the flak was worse. Everybody had to take a turn at these fields and I don't suppose our turn came up any more often than any other crew's. It just seemed that way.

We supposed our trips coincided with bomber attacks on Berlin, Hamburg, Bremen, or Hannover or all four of them. In any case, the airfields we patrolled stretched in a wide band from the Dutch-German border almost to Berlin: Twente (in Holland), Rheine, Plantlunne, Achmer, Hesepe, Quakenbruck, Varrel Busch, Ahlhorn, Vechta, Diepholz, Bomlitz, Munster, Fassberg, Celle, Gardelegen, Stendal. Small-town Germany was as nasty in its own way as citified Germany. The trouble was, the heavies never dropped their loads on the small towns and their nearby fighter dromes, except by accident; when we showed up in our shadow role, all these fields were as fresh as daisies and ready to take us on. Their nerves had seldom been stretched by air-raid sirens.

Another problem was that there were Canadian and British radar-equipped night fighters around. They didn't have to see you to find you. Their radar latched onto you and sometimes the guys with the radar were a little trigger-happy and shot before they were absolutely, positively, dead certain of the identity of the guy on the other end. Who needed friends like these? There were recurrent stories in the Chez Moi that some of the night fighter aces had built their scores by not being too choosy about their targets. Dead men tell no tales, especially about friends. No wonder the ass-end Charlies in the bombers shot first and asked their questions, if any, afterwards. The guts of too many tail gunners had been hosed out of rear turrets.

I had one hell of a time finding all these airfields. We were assigned two or three for a night's work, but often Sid felt like dropping in on a couple of others on the way home. It was a little difficult to drop in when I didn't know exactly where we were when he decided on an extra visit.

The first part was easy. We entered by the same route every time we were on these Berlin zone intruder trips: over a little seaside village on the Dutch coast, Egmond aan Zee. I guess the Dutch got used to our entry point and time because one night, just as we crossed the white line where the North Sea met the sand, a window was thrown up, somebody leaned out and waved both arms. Was the person arrested for making a flaw in the blackout? Or shot for signalling the enemy? Or was it husband or wife seeking a desperate lungful of air in the middle of a family fight? Anyway, I waved back.

We flew straight across the Zeider Zee and on the east side followed the perfectly straight line of land formed by the southern edge of the northeast polder, or reclaimed land. So much more of the Zeider Zee has been reclaimed, I suppose it would be impossible to find the same landmarks today. From the Zee we flew east to the Ems canal, which had some good twists in it for pinpoint purposes. It's almost as if the canal builders had a lost soul like me in mind.

My next pinpoint after the Ems Canal was Dummer Lake, about twenty-five miles southwest of Bremen. On the map, it stood out like an enormous blue thumb. Better still, there wasn't supposed to be any flak near it.

The only trouble with Dummer Lake was that I never saw it, not once. I haven't seen it to this day. Was it a dummy lake, like the dummy airfield near Munich? Or did Jerry cover it over every night with a tarpaulin? My fellow navigators claimed they often used it as a pinpoint and had seen it. But when I questioned them closely, I found them to be a little evasive. Was it really a rectangle as shown on the map? Well, not quite a rectangle. Were there an autobahn and railway on the east side? Well, maybe a bit more to the south rather than east. Did any streams run into it? Well, nothing very big. Was there a town on the south side? Well, more a cluster of houses, one would say.

I used the damn lake five times as a pinpoint before I gave up in frustration. I daubed it in red and told Sid there was a flak island in the middle of the lake. He was easy because he'd never seen the lake either. We settled on Steinhuder Lake, farther east, but we seldom saw it. We tried to spot the Weser Canal and groped our way around as best as we could from there. To say that I knew even roughly where we were over Germany all the time would be a wild exaggeration. In fact, those were the very words used by Sid in the mess.

Sid wanted almost desperately to shoot down a plane but if he could see anything at all moving on the ground in the form of trucks or trains, he didn't hang around an unlighted and inactive airfield.

"Why in hell don't we ever see a plane?" he would ask rhetorically. Then, a few minutes later: "Christ, they're all asleep here. Let's go over to that other field, what'sitsname."

Often, on the way to the new target, he'd spot a train. Why we saw so many trains and so few planes I couldn't imagine. Sid didn't always go at the trains broadside as he had on that Munich trip. None of them ever sat up as pretty as that one had. Usually, we caught them in a cut and this forced us to go at them lengthways. We came off second best only once: a flak car shot back at us and we went home with one engine.

"Jesus," I said, after we were safely down, "you land on one engine more often than most pilots land on two."

"Well, I still got you home early."

He was right. We'd stopped the train on the way in and were spared two hours lurking about a fighter field waiting for some unheeding clod to put his lights on in the circuit. Even at 180 miles an hour instead of 240, we were back before the Turkey Cock closed. That was one of the benefits of early nightfall in the autumn.

Another night, soon after we ambushed a train between Rheine and Lingen, we were comfortably out over the North Sea on the way home when the English coast failed to show up. Another five minutes and still no English coast. Even with my navigation, you could hardly miss England altogether. It should be there, a great big island, right in our path.

"Well?" Sid said.

I started to think hard. The weather was good and we'd seen the Dutch coast on our way out. The course was set properly on the compass. The elapsed time should have brought us to the coast five minutes before. There was little wind. Anyway, even a wind head-on affected us very little at low-level.

"Do you want me to fly this course till we run out of gas?" Sid asked.

I thought: if we somehow had turned south, we would have hit France. If we'd gone west, we'd be home. If we'd gone east, we'd be back over Germany and probably aware of it because Germany wasn't ocean and we were over ocean. Therefore, I said to myself, we've flown north.

"Turn ninety degrees port," I told Sid.

"That's quite a change, even for you," he said, but he

pulled us around to the left. A moment later he said: "Check the gas." We were OK.

"Look out the back." I turned around. "How long on this leg?" Sid asked.

"Half an hour anyway," I said.

"Where does that put us? Over Berlin or Ireland?"

Jesus, what a smart-ass. There was a twenty-five minute silence.

"Turn port some more," I said, "about thirty degrees."

"Whee," Sid said. If he was worried, he didn't give any sign of it. A few minutes later, we hit the English coast at Newcastle and flew south to Hunsdon.

"What happened?" Sid asked.

"It was all your fault," I said. "When you fired the cannons at that train, it knocked the compass out of kilter. It's out at least ninety degrees."

"How did you figure that out?"

"Smart." I didn't tell him that Jimmy Gibbons, our squadron navigator, had told me in the mess a few nights before that he had got caught with a screwy compass and had nearly gone crazy figuring his way back from Magdeburg.

"Get a load of my alligator's latest alibi," Sid told the mess. "We fire. No compass. Can't get home. We're halfway to the North Pole and running out of gas and he finally tells me to fly west."

Jimmy was about to say something to Sid, looked at me, smiled handsomely and said nothing. Another friend for life, except that Jimmy didn't have long to live.

A few nights later, we were again over the Zeider Zee when Sid spotted three small ships. He pulled around to port and got lined up quickly for a run at them.

"Attacking shipping is not our business," I said primly.

"Well, it's my business. You can get out if you want."

We went in with the cannons clattering and the machine guns spitting. We hit the deck of one ship from a fair distance and Sid turned slightly to starboard and hit the second one. There were sparks as our shells hit metal and pieces of wood flew off. On our second run, Sid pasted the small ship we hadn't attacked on the first go and got a lick in at one of the others. Our stuff was ricocheting all over the place.

I wasn't any more scared than I normally was, until I got a good look at the deck of one of the ships where a small fire was starting up. There were some guys running around on deck and they were unlimbering some kind of a gun. Jesus they had a nerve to shoot back at us.

What I had to do was stop a third run by Sid. Mention of a gun which hadn't fired wouldn't deter him. After all, we'd been shot at before. It was the accepted practice. What scared Sid, if anything?

Searchlights! They put the wind up him. But there weren't likely to be any searchlights on three small ships in the middle of the Zeider Zee. I had to think of something else.

Every pilot was alarmed at the possibility of being caught in a balloon barrage. A couple of our guys had run into the London balloon barrage during the doodlebug siege. One made it back with a piece of wing off. The other didn't.

"Balloons!" I shouted. We were just coming around for another pass.

"What? Where?"

"One of those ships was just getting one up when we made our last run."

"Which ship?"

"I don't know. I'm turned around now."

Sid peered down. A bit of moonlight was filtering through the overcast, mixing and weaving shadow and darkness.

"Christ those balloons are hard to see," Sid said.

"They sure are," I said. "They look just like the water."

"Well, we'll try one more pass," Sid said.

I decided to give it one more try. Sid was beginning a shallow dive. "There it is," I shouted. "Pull starboard."

Sid yanked us to the right.

"God that was close," I said.

"What, what?"

"Didn't you see it? About 100 feet up. The cable would have cut us right in two."

"You have real sharp eyes tonight," Sid said. "You must have been feeding your rods carrots."

Rods were the name of the thing in your eyes which was supposed to help night vision. Nearly every time Sid came in out of the blackout he would exclaim, "My God, my rods."

"Tricky in that light," I offered.

He levelled out and then turned onto the compass heading we'd been on before the encounter.

When we were having our tatty piece of liver and greasy egg, Sid leaned over and said: "C'mon, Dave, was there really a balloon there?"

I looked him straight in the eye and said: "Would I kid you, Sid?" This was real serious stuff. We didn't call each other Sid and Dave very often. He called me "boy" and I called him "champ".

"You're a lying son of a bitch," he said.

"Your mother wrote and asked me to look after you," I said.

"Goddam it, McIntosh, you're impossible."

"And you're still healthy."

"Let's go."

We went over to the ops room and saw the IO and claimed three small ships damaged.

"What kind of ships?" the IO asked.

"I don't know," Sid said. "A balloon got in the way and we couldn't identify them properly."

And we went out and got in the truck and went home to bed.

The talk of the ops room the next afternoon was about a plane which radar had tracked as it circled for more than two hours about twenty miles off the Dutch coast. Radar followed the plane as it flew to England and to Hunsdon.

One of our crews had been so lacking in moral fibre — that was the official phrase—that they had done nearly half a tour circling off the enemy coast. The navigator had cooked up a log noting targets visited, burning bombers, fires, weather, the whole thing. The pair would have finished a tour that way if the radar hadn't been randomly spotting that night at very low level.

The two men were already gone. There were no announcements, no court martial.

"God, what they went through," Sid said. I understood what he meant, but Henderson didn't. He would have to be told, as usual.

"They were chicken," Henderson said.

"Imagine how scared they were," Sid said. "And not only afraid of Germans. Think how frightened they were of being found out. They didn't even know the relief of getting back from a trip because their work really only began then, lying to the IO, hoping they hadn't been spotted, fearing some little detail would trip them up. Think of spending two and three and four hours making up a log, putting in all the times, going over it again and again, over there in the dark flying around and around and around."

"Bullshit, they were just plain fucking chicken," Henderson said.

Some people never understand, even when you tell them.

Sid leaned over to me and said in a stage whisper, "At least that was one navigator who worked his ass off." I took it in goods spirits. I always could, when I was sitting there, safe and sound.

Sid went down to London for a day right after our "Big Ben" incident.

Big Ben was the code word for the V-2, the Jerry rocket which went sixty or seventy miles into the air and fell on London or anywhere where it felt like coming down. (I could understand there being code words for our secret weapons, but why we had them for theirs baffled me. The Germans already knew about their own secret weapons.)

A V-2 hit near our house one night when we were

ooling our parcels from home for a big feed of Klik, Klak,
luk and canned pineapple. There was this great big
xplosion, then a rumble. The rumble was its own noise
atching up to it. Anyway, they had us up looking for Big Ben
aunching sites for God's sake. Whoosh, a ball of fire, and
aat was that. Sid and I didn't even see one.

We were uselessly stooging around somewhere in
olland, when this limey voice said into our earphones:
Waggle your wings, you bastard, or you'll burn."

We waggled. Wildly. The Mosquito nearly turned inside
ut.

"OK, son," came the same voice. A Brit night fighter
ith radar had crawled right up our old chuff.

"That dirty, rotten, lousy, Jew-baiting son of a bitch,"
d said.

My mouth was wide open again, as usual, and I
as trying to get it shut and make my vocal cords work.
nally, I managed to say, "Thank God our receiver was
orking."

"By Jesus, I'd shoot that son of a bitch down if I could
e him," Sid threatened.

The remark reminded me later of General Patton's
npatient jab at the Canadians and Brits for being so slow
osing the Falaise Gap in Normandy: "Get those goddam
rits out of my way or I'll Dunkirk 'em."

A moment later, Sid said, "Screw this night work."

The next morning, he went to London. I knew what he
as up to. He was seeing Intelligence to find out where he
ould go to find a whole lot of Jerry planes in daylight. He
me back that evening, looking triumphant.

"We're going to Norway," he announced. "Bags of stuff
there."

I was horrified, naturally. Some of our guys were going
Czechoslovakia in daylight. I hadn't bargained on
ything worse than that, though that was bad enough.

"You can't fly up those goddam fiords," I said. "They
ve nothing but guns on both sides."

"But I have a plan," Sid said. There was no putting him off. "We're going in behind Oslo."

"But you can't fly up Oslo fiord," I protested.

"We're going around it. Overland."

And that's what we did. Morey and Fred came with us and flew No. 2.

It took us three hops to get to Norway. We flew to Leuchars in Scotland to refuel and then to Wick near the top of Scotland to stop overnight. It was raining and cold. Wick was a coastal command base and the squadrons there had spent years looking for submarines.

We set out for Oslo the next morning, flying almost due east. The weather cleared, far too much. There wasn't a cloud as we skirted the southern tip of Norway and ducked inland well south of Oslo. We threaded our way in and out of the valleys. Near Drammen, we came over a mountain ridge suddenly and found ourselves sitting like ducks more than 1,000 feet above a huge valley floor.

Sid dove down the side of the ridge, across the valley floor. We swept up the other side but the ridge was more than we expected. We barely staggered over the top.

"See if Morey made it," Sid said. Morey was right behind, to starboard.

We continued straight north, cut due east again behind Oslo, then due south again for an airfield near Fredrikstad. We would be taking the base from the rear and we had come one hell of a long way to do it.

"They'll never guess we're here," Sid said, practically rubbing his hands together in glee. Intelligence had told him the base was packed with Jerry planes.

We flew to the east side of the field—Sweden was even closer than it had been at Malmo—and came in together. We got a bit of height so that we could dive to the attack and had a hard look around.

Nothing. Zero. Goose egg. Shutout. There wasn't one goddam single plane on the field. We flew right down the main runway. On the far side of the field was a big, open hangar and out in front of it was one lone guy in uniform. Even the hangar was empty.

"I'll be a son of a bitch," Sid said.

The guy was running.

Sid gave him all cannons and machine guns. Morey gave him the same. Chips of cement flew all around the guy. There was a cloud of cement dust. I looked back as we swept by the hangar and pulled up. The guy was still running like a deer. We hadn't laid a glove on him. I thought it best not to tell Sid then.

Morey called up: "Was that it?"

Sid didn't reply.

Why did we keep running into these odd individuals like this? There was the guy at Vaerlose who fell off a ladder, the fisherman who tried to gun us down in broad daylight from his boat, the man or woman who flung up a window in greeting on the Dutch coast, now this track star in Norway. Where in hell did they come from? What in hell were they doing there just as we came along? Whom would we meet next like this?

We went back the way we came in, behind Oslo to avoid the fiord, then down the valleys toward the south coast. Sid had planned to drop in on one more field, so we steered for it. It was beside a long, narrow lake in a long narrow valley in the mountains north of Kristiansand. We found the place all right. We roared down the valley and beside the lake we found a hut and a grass runway. No planes, not even a hangar this time.

Morey called up again: "Jesus, Sid."

Sid didn't reply. He said to me: "How can I ever face him?"

A little later, he said, "Any more daylights we'll do alone."

We reached a narrow valley and flew between two cliffsides. "Do you know what Intelligence told me?" Sid asked.

"You mean about all those planes parked at that field?"

"No, not that. They told me to be damn careful flying in these Norwegian fiords and valleys. The Jerries string cables across some of the canyons." Thank God he had saved that one until we were nearly out.

We came out over Kristiansand. Sid was so disgusted that he neglected to shoot down the mountainside and out over the sea at low level and high speed. But he shoved the throttles forward when the heavy flak opened up. There were black bursts behind us. The gunners must have been startled by our unannounced appearance and their aim was off.

We landed at Peterhead about 1330 after a five-hour scenic tour, refuelled, and flew on to Hunsdon.

Sid told the intelligence officer he could tell his superiors in London what he thought about them. We all crept back to the mess and Sid bought the drinks.

"Sorry, Morey," he said again.

"In peacetime you'd pay hundreds of dollars for a trip like that," Morey said. He and Fred and I were just glad to be back.

There was some scotch. Sid bought eight scotches and put them all in one big glass. After a while he began to feel better. He called Jack over.

"Hey, you want a hot tip on where to get good gen on where Jerry parks his planes? Well, I met this Brit groupie in London. A secret rendezvous. And he tells me that there's this little hidden field in Norway with hundreds, yes hundreds, of FWs and MEs and transports, everything . . ."

By the time he got to our unrelenting hunt for the enemy on a grass runway beside a hut on the shore of a beautiful lake with cables crisscrossing box canyons at either end, he was in full flight for the evening.

The CO came in late. He was so fascinated with the saga that he ordered the bar kept open. I didn't even think very much about the next daylight trip.

It didn't take long for Sid to pick a new daylight target and get permission from Russ to go. "Kolberg," Sid told me.

He pointed it out on the big map covering one wall of the ops room. It was on the Baltic coast, in what today is Poland. We'd look at a couple of other fields on the way in. And we'd go alone.

"Can we get that far?" I asked.

Sid had it all figured out. We'd refuel at a Belgian field which had been taken over by the Americans or British. We'd take off before dawn and catch sleeping Jerry at first light.

"This time we'll find some planes," Sid announced.

All I could do was swallow hard.

I drew a route across the Elbe and north of Berlin to the fields we were going to visit. But I concentrated on the exit route. I had a homeward route from points every few miles along our track. I wrote the courses and times for these routes right on the map so that when I got the shakes I wouldn't have to hunt them up on my log with my palsied fingers.

We were walking out to the dispersal the next afternoon to fly to Belgium, when Russ Bannock went by in his tiny staff car. He stopped, and leaned out of the window. "Good luck," he said.

He beckoned me back as Sid walked on toward the plane. "Look after him," Russ said.

In all the war, it was the most magnificent sentence I heard or read. I was so moved all I could mumble was, "Yes, sir." I'd never before addressed Russ as sir though he was the CO.

"What did he want?" Sid asked.

"He told me to goddam well smarten up in my navigation."

"You're lying again, boy."

"Yes." I let it go at that.

I peed under the port wing and we flew to Le Culot in Belgium, taking our ladder with us, neatly folded up.

There wasn't a plane on the field. "Must still belong to the Jerries," Sid said.

We parked near a hangar whose roof had been bombed in. I extended the ladder and we got out. Somebody was picking through the rubble. He was also carrying a rifle. Sid was going to haul out his pistol, but thought better of it. When he felt real swashbuckling, he wore his pistol. I never wore mine. I was afraid I might wound myself. I had never even fired a practice round.

The guy kept his rifle slung over his shoulder.

"Where is everybody?" Sid asked.

"Le toit rouge," the Belgian replied.

"OK," Sid said to me, "You're from Quebec."

"The building with the red roof, dummy," I said. For good measure, I turned to the Belgian and said, "Merci bien, monsieur."

"There are some advantages to travelling with a man of culture," Sid said.

We found a lone American sergeant under the red roof. He was from an engineering unit. No, there was no American or RAF or any other squadron in those parts. A limey outfit had left the day before. I was going to remind Sid of his brilliant Oslo attack plan but decided to hold my tongue.

"All we need is some gas," Sid said.

The sergeant got on his radio phone and summoned a jeep, which took us to a big house in a wood where an American captain introduced himself. "Leave it to me," he said.

We needed aviation gas, not the truck gas this outfit had. The captain got on the phone while Sid kept telling everybody that came in and went out that he might be wearing this silly blue uniform but he was really an American from San Francisco.

"You don't say" or "Well, goddam" they said.

After a while, the captain said: "Let's go down to the field." When we got there, there was a bowser parked beside the Mosquito and putting in gas.

"There's another little thing," Sid said.

"I know," replied the captain, a huge man with a big gut hanging over his belt, "there's no flarepath."

He and Sid took the jeep over to the runway. It had been

bombed and repaired, but there were still bomb craters on either side. They came back and Sid told me: "He'll fix everything."

We went back to the big house and the captain ordered bacon and eggs for us. He had two cots put up in his office. The blankets were dry. They were the first dry blankets I'd seen since leaving Canada.

"I'll get you up in time," the captain said. He moved his table out into the hall and shut the door. "I want quiet," he told his underlings.

For the first time in our tour — this was trip No. 39 — I couldn't sleep. It was the middle of October and cold, but I couldn't sleep for the sweat. Sid slept like a baby.

I pretended to be asleep when the captain shook us awake at 0330. He drove us to the plane. It was as black as pitch. He ignored the blackout and ordered the gas bowser to park at the end of the runway so that its lights would guide our takeoff.

"Take off before you reach the lights," he said.

I thought Sid would say something like, "What a splendid idea." But all he said was, "Yes."

"Now I'll put the jeep on the other side with its lights shining along the runway," said the captain. "This way you'll know where the center of the runway is and the bowser lights will show you where the end is."

"Yes," said Sid.

We climbed in and the captain handed our ladder up to us. "Here's a little present for the way back," he said. He handed me a big round can. There was no label on it. "It's sausages," the captain said.

He handed me a slip of paper. "And here's our address. Write us if you make it back."

I put the paper in my tunic and the can behind Sid's seat on top of the Gee set.

The captain led us to the starting end of the runway with his jeep, then went ahead and parked about halfway down the runway. The bowser lights shone faintly in the distance across the runway.

"You call the headings," Sid said. Sid pushed the throttles ahead and we picked up speed slowly.

"Two-sixty," I said, the reading on the gyro compass and the direction of the runway.

More speed.

"Two-sixty-two." Sid eased the Mosquito back to port a bit.

"Two-sixty."

We flashed by the jeep.

"Two-sixty."

Sid pulled back just before we reached the bowser lights and we were off. I looked back and the bowser lights blinked off and then on again.

"Nice guys," Sid said. "Americans."

I gave him the course for the Elbe and he put it on the compass. We flew higher than we normally did because we wanted to be sure where we were when dawn broke and we went down on the deck. Sid had said if we didn't find our exact pinpoint on the Elbe he'd fly north to the North Sea and we'd go home. He'd never put such temptation in front of me before.

Was there once a book called *Hold Back the Dawn*? I tried to hold back that beautiful October dawn, but it just kept coming. There was haze and then shreds of ground fog as light began to show. In the distance I could easily make out the Elbe. We didn't see a plane or train or truck or car or anything moving. Germany seemed deserted.

"OK, start down," I said. I was aiming not only for a bend in the Elbe, but a particularly odd bend, with an island to boot. There was no way to confuse it with any other turn in the river.

We were at 500 feet when I spotted the pinpoint. I was glad and afraid at the same time, glad that I hadn't let Sid down and afraid because now we'd have to go the rest of the way.

"Circle once," I said.

"Are you lost already?" Sid said.

"Just check-check," I said. We went around in a wide turn. That was it all right, the bend, the island, the road, the railway track, the village, everything.

"OK," I said, "Let's get right down." Back to graveyard flying. I gave Sid the new course, slightly north of due east. It was up to him to follow it as accurately as possible. If we wandered from it, we'd be lost.

It was eight minutes to Muritz Lake, our next pinpoint. There was a lot of fog, but it was patchy, enabling me to read the ground and keep track of where we were. Rechlin airfield was on the south shore of Muritz Lake. We did an orbit but couldn't see any planes. We continued east for six minutes to an unnamed lake just south of a big airfield at Prenzlau. Again, nothing.

"Christ, another Oslo," said Sid.

"We still haven't reached our target," I said.

I put the Berlin map on the bottom of my pile and spread out the Stettin map. Five and a half minutes to Madu Lake, ten miles southeast of Stettin. We were still going east. My God, we were a long way from home.

We crossed the narrow lake until we hit a railway line. We turned north and in less than a minute we were at Stargard airfield. The first thing I saw was a Jerry plane, a Messerschmitt 110. Before I could say anything, Sid had let off a one-second burst of cannon fire. I could see the shells hitting home and yellow flames came out of the wing roots, followed by a huge puff of black smoke.

The second thing I saw was a parade, maybe a church parade. After all, it was Sunday morning. At least a hundred guys were drawn up in perfect lines in the middle of the field. The moment they heard our cannon, they broke and ran, stumbling, falling over each other, crawling on hands and knees, but all moving. For a change, it wasn't just one guy in our line of fire.

There were about a dozen Me-109s parked at the far side

of the field. Sid couldn't get a crack at them because we'd seen them too late. He yanked back on the stick, we tore up to 700 feet and did a stall turn. While I played my usual role of mute and terrified witness, Sid closed to fifty yards with a two-second burst. One Me-109 exploded immediately. Sid hit two others. In the same instant, he spotted two more planes on the south side of the field, one of them a Stuka. He got in a quick burst just as we started going over on our port side, and the Stuka exploded. There were hits on another plane beside it.

There wasn't really room to manoeuvre in making this last attack. We were only twenty feet or so off the deck and when Sid went to correct our roll to port, we stalled. The goddam stick flew right out of Sid's hand. I watched in fascinated horror: Sid's hand in one place, the stick in another. We were obviously going to smash right into the deck in another split second. There wouldn't even be time for a "dear God" and scream let alone a final statement for posterity.

But the plane in one flick righted itself. The stick found Sid's hand. We were flying straight and level at about ten feet over an open field.

In my relief, I became furious. "What in hell do you think you're flying, a yoyo?" I shouted.

"Count the columns of smoke," Sid said.

I counted five columns, rising as high as 200 feet.

"How many did we destroy?" Sid asked.

"You haven't answered my question about flying a yoyo," I said. This was bold. But I was mad as hell. There we were practically upside down over a Jerry airfield and my pilot isn't even holding the stick.

"I bet I get a personal interview with P.J.," Sid said. And he laughed at his own lousy joke.

Every Mosquito combat report went to P.J. de Havilland, Esq. P.J. was one of thirteen destinations for our combat reports but not one of them was the RCAF. It is still hard to believe that RCAF headquarters pulled its forelock so hard and so often to the RAF that it couldn't even be put on the mailing list for combat reports from its own squadrons.

I gave Sid a 038 degrees course for our next pinpoint, a clearing in the middle of a wood five minutes away. We were going north but still veering to the east, farther than ever from home.

"Let's review this," Sid said. "You put it down in the log."

"First," Sid recounted, "there was the Me-110 right at the start. It burned. One destroyed. Then, on the second run, we hit three Me-109s. One exploded. That's two destroyed. What happened to the other two?"

"I don't know. I didn't see them burn."

"You said you counted five columns of smoke."

"I did, but one might have been the cookhouse."

"You're pretty smart for seven in the morning."

"I got wakened up when I saw us flying without you holding the stick."

"There, there."

This exchange is going on while I'm trying to read the ground and Sid is hugging the deck. Jerry knows we're around but he doesn't know what direction we've taken, I hope.

"Those last two," Sid said. "One was a Stuka. It exploded. What was the other thing with two engines?"

"I haven't a clue, but we hit it."

"Put down three destroyed and three damaged then," Sid said. "How far is Kolberg?"

"Four minutes after this pinpoint, if we see it," I said.

The fog had cleared by this time. The day was beautiful and crisp and clear and cloudless. The Mosquito's shadow ran over the sunlit trees. We arrived at the clearing in the wood and I told Sid to change course fifteen degrees to port.

"You're hot today, boy," he said. That mollified me considerably.

When we hit the road and railway near the coast, we turned west and flew down the railway track to Kolberg airfield. Sid pulled up to 300 feet. Nearly all the hangars control tower, and other buildings were on the south side of the field, to our left. In front of us were parked two Junkers 88s. Sid opened up at 100 yards with a one-second squeeze on the button. He hit the wing roots of one of them and flame and smoke came out. Four more Ju-88s were parked in front of the hangars. Sid pulled up slightly, dived and attacked again. He hit two of them and one started to burn.

I looked for some kind of Jerry activity, such as ack-ack guns. But there wasn't a soul outside. After all, it was 0703, still on a Sunday morning.

Sid and I both spotted another bunch of planes parked at the northwest side of the field. This time, he didn't try to turn the Mosquito into a pretzel to get at them.

"Shall we take another run?" Sid asked. That little business of being a pilot without a stick seemed to have impressed him to the point of asking my opinion.

"OK," I said. I couldn't believe my own mouth. But it sure was peaceful. I forgot at that moment — I thought of it later — that perhaps Stargard had ordered up some fighters to cut off our flight west.

Sid did an orbit around the field, just as if we were getting ready to land at Hunsdon, and we again attacked out of a brilliant sun. Sid picked the plane beside the first one he had attacked which had begun to burn. He set it afire. Then he went for the same second group in front of the hangars. It was like watching a rerun. One Ju-88 exploded. Sid pulled up sharply, twisted to starboard and got in a burst at the third group of Ju-88s. We could see the shells hit and pieces fly off, but nothing else happened. Just as we pulled away, one of them blew up.

We didn't have a chance to do any counting because a few seconds later we ran into a flock of birds. Thump, thump, thump. There was blood and feathers all over the windscreen.

"I can't see," Sid said. "I'll have to pull up a bit."

I didn't like that. We were right out there in the open for all to see.

Sid got the wipers and windscreen spray working but it was three or four minutes before the screen was clear enough for Sid to get back down on the deck.

"Funny flak they've got here," Sid said.

A minute later, we were approaching the town of Cammin just before we turned northwest over the sea for Denmark. A tall building loomed up in front of us. It must have been ten storeys high and was right in front of us. It must about the sixth storey, there was somebody out on a balcony. He was sitting in a chair and had one leg propped up on another chair. The leg was covered in what I took to be a cast.

"That son of a bitch is right in our way," Sid said. He punched the machine-gun button, just one little squirt. The bullets hit the brick but not the man on the balcony.

Sid banked around the building.

"Was that a hospital?" I asked.

"Christ, no," Sid said.

I hadn't seen any Red Cross markings and I'm sure Sid hadn't. But it was odd, that guy in a cast on the balcony.

We didn't speak of it again. We flew across Rugen, then Laaland and Langeland and came out at our old familiar spot north of Romo. We didn't see a thing except the autumn colours of the Danish countryside and still, blue, sparkling water.

We did another tally and put down five destroyed and two damaged at Kolberg. That made eight destroyed and five damaged altogether for the two airfields.

Then Sid said, "It's time for the sausages." I had forgotten them. I fished out the can from behind his seat.

"We don't have an opener."

"Yes, we do." Sid produced a knife from his flying boot.

I had to stab the can in several places before I could make an opening big enough to extract the sausages, one at a time. They were packed in butter or margarine and were skinless.

"You can rely on the Yanks," Sid said. They were the greatest sausages I have ever eaten.

Save some for the ground crew," Sid said.

When we arrived over the English coast, a Spitfire drew alongside to look us over. The pilot pointed toward our wings but we weren't on his radio channel, so couldn't make conversation.

I held up eight fingers and wondered if the Spit pilot could make eight planes destroyed out of the signal.

"Cut it out," Sid said. "They were all on the ground, for Christ's sake." The bastard was never satisfied.

We landed at 1025 and Hal had his familiar question as soon as he opened the door: "What in hell happened?"

"Some birds bombed us," Sid said.

We climbed down the ladder and took a look. There were five big holes in the wings and tail and a big dent in the nose.

"Give me a screwdriver," Sid said to Hal. He took the film container out and carried it to the dispersal hut. He found a pair of scissors, fed out the end of film, snipped it off and put it in his pocket. That was the part showing a guy in a cast on a balcony.

Neither of us said anything.

Russ was so pleased with our trip he had it announced on the PA system in the mess at Sunday lunch.

Sid and I went down to London next day to make a recording for the CBC. We spent all day in the pub with Bing Whittaker and two RCAF public relations officers. It was a great day for drinking but not much for script-writing. Nobody was allowed simply to speak into the microphone. It all had to be scripted. Bing entertained grandly while the two PROs took turns writing a few lines in some nearby office. In its completed form, the script had Sid and I throwing the conversational ball to each other by ending every sentence with "Eh, Sid?" or "Eh, Dave?" Everybody had a good time and our mothers adored the recording.

I was already living on borrowed time. My life, and Sid's, should have ended when that stick flew out of his hands over Stargard. From here on, every day of my life was gravy.

Sid wrote to the captain at Le Culot, as Yank to Yank, of course. He gave him our score and thanked him for the sausages. We never heard back.

CHAPTER NINE

When we got back from leave, we were assigned Kassel on the night of November 11, Armistice Day. My mother and my sister would have already trudged to Crystal Lake Cemetery in Stanstead to place a wreath of poppies on my father's gravestone. Despite the foul weather, all twelve crews were on duty for "flowers" all over Germany.

Sid hadn't had a chance to tell everybody about Kolberg before we went on leave, so he addressed the usual audience — some old faces gone forever, some new ones added — gathered around the sputtering stove.

"You wouldn't believe the goddam abuse I have to take from my alligator. 'What in hell do you think you're flying, a yoyo?' he says to me with more brass than Flash Gordon. And just because we're over on our back, ten feet off the deck and the stick flies out of my hand. I mean, none of you guys would put up with shit like that from your alligator."

He looked at Jack and Morey and the other pilots. If there was ever another pilot who said right out loud he'd stalled on the deck so that the stick had flown out of his hand, I've never heard of him.

Sid composed as he went. "My alligator says he doesn't want me to touch the stick from now on. Right, boy? He says I fly a hell of a lot better by letting the machinery do all the work. I said he could go alone but he says he hates to sit and watch scenery all by himself.

"Well, my boy here can navigate circles around any of your alligators. If he doesn't take me right over a burning city, he takes me right into a flock of birds. It's not easy to find a flock of birds like that."

This would be our fortieth operational trip together. I still slept well, ate badly, drank a lot and kept my weight at 133 on my six-foot one-inch frame. A rag, a bone, and three exposed nerve ends. We didn't have far to go now to finish a tour. Two, three, or four or maybe five trips. It wasn't a finite number of trips on 418 squadron. It was when the CO figured you'd done your share and that if you did any more you might get too tired and make a fatal mistake. It was a fine line.

There was always the chance of the fatal mistake. Experience helped, but it wasn't everything. You had to be lucky, too. Guys often bought it on their third or fourth tours. Nearly half the guys Sid and I had started with were dead or missing. From the ones we knew who had been screened — that is, told their tours were finished — we gathered that Russ seemed to err on the side of one fewer trip rather than one extra. Bless him.

"Come on, chicken," Sid said. We got our gear and went outside. It was a damp, cold, cloudy night, black as ink, and not yet 1800 hours.

By the time we got to the Dutch coast, we were bouncing all over the sky. We couldn't see a thing. I only guessed we had crossed the coast.

"We'll never find Kassel in this crap," I said.

"We're going," Sid pronounced.

We flew up and down like a bird in a chimney. The storm pitched us all over the place.

"We might as well turn back. It's no disgrace in weather like this," I pointed out.

"We'll get through this front before long," Sid said.

We did, but it wasn't any better for navigation. There was nothing but cloud and Sid had to increase our altitude because we weren't sure whether there was high ground where we were.

He kept climbing higher.

"You're going to fly this plane. I have to pee," Sid said. How in hell could he think up these new wrinkles to scare me?

He fished around with his left hand and found the pilot's tube for leaking. I always resented that there was no similar equipment on the navigator's side. You'd think de Havilland might have guessed that navigators had to pee, too.

Sid unhooked his straps and got his fly open and the funnel of the tube in the proper position. "Now hold the stick, and make goddam sure you grab the right one." He should have been playing the Palladium.

I took the stick gingerly.

"It won't bite you," Sid said.

I had to lean over farther. As I did so, all my maps slipped off my lap and onto the floor.

Sid held the funnel of the tube with his left hand and his penis with his right.

"You're going over to port," Sid said.

I pulled the stick slightly to the right. The guy who had spun a Link ground trainer was flying over an armed Germany.

"Christ," Sid said, "the tube's plugged."

I looked. The funnel was full to the brim and nothing was disappearing down the tube.

We started going over to port again.

"Pull her back," Sid shouted.

I was so startled I pushed to the left instead of the right. We really started over.

"Get away," Sid yelled. He dropped the funnel and grabbed the stick.

The full load of the funnel and the tube down to the point where it was plugged went all over my feet and the maps.

"Where are we?" Sid said.

The dirty rotten evil-smelling bastard. I contemplated the floor for some time. There was no way around it. I would have to pick up those maps. My log was down there, too.

I shoved the maps around with my feet, loosened my straps, picked up one map by the corner between two fingernails and put it as far out on my knees as I could and still be able to read it with my flashlight with its beam no bigger round than a pin.

We flew on in the cloud to where we thought Kassel might be and did a north-south patrol in cloud for two hours, bumping along like a stone boat.

We flew back through the front, riding the elevator swiftly up and down. Sid never bitched. He just bored ahead, flying every second, never relaxing.

When we got home and the Mosquito hatch opened, Hal said, "Which one of you guys pissed his pants?"

Sid got a couple of burlap bags in the flight hut and wiped up the mess. He wasn't the kind of guy who would leave a job like that for the ground crew. Maybe me, but not the ground crew.

I was going to throw away all the maps immediately. Then, I thought, they've carried me this far, it would be bad luck to discard them, like forgetting to pee under the port wing before takeoff. I wished Sid had adopted that superstition.

The air which always blew around the cockpit and up my pantlegs because I wore shoes and not flight boots had helped to dry off the maps. I put them in my canvas bag and took them back to the ops room.

Oddly, all the crews were in the ops room. We'd never seen this before. Usually, the crews went home by twos and threes soon after they reported to the IO.

"Christ, we thought you'd gone for the chop," Jack said.

I suddenly realized what had happened. Everybody else had sensibly turned back because of the awful weather. They all presumed we'd flown into the ground or been shot down.

The pilots gathered around Sid and clapped him on the back. I don't think he realized at first what a rare tribute it was for all the crews to wait up for one lone stray. I hadn't seen anything like it since we had all gathered around outside to watch Jas and Archie coming in from that day ranger with a hole in the tailplane so big you could drive an Austin through it.

They had been really worried about Sid. They had wanted him to come back.

Some of the navigators went up to him and said, "Nice going, Sid." They recognized, too, that he had done some professional flying to go through that front twice.

"How did you get through that stuff?" George asked me.

"Routine for my boy," I said.

We all piled into the trucks and cars and drove to the mess, where Russ opened the bar.

Op. 41 took us to Delmenhorst and Lemwerden on the outskirts of Bremen. I didn't like any target but I especially didn't like them near cities which had been bombed repeatedly. The flak gunners had had lots of practice.

We followed our usual route into Europe over the Zeider Zee and Sid made the usual remark that, this time, surely to God, we'd see a Jerry plane in the air with its lights on.

We skirted to the north of Ahlhorn, Varrel Busch, and Bissel and started a patrol just west of Bremen, flying north and south between the two target airfields. Twice, a stream of orange tennis balls came up. I thought they were going to scorch my privates but they missed them and the plane. We all had a nagging fear that our jewels might be shot off. J.P. caught a shell in his inner leg right beside his balls. His navigator, Bernie, shot the morphine to him to kill the pain and somehow managed not to give him too much. As a result, J.P. didn't pass out and got them home. Pilots had a steel plate under their seats to protect them. Navigators had an extra sheet of plywood. The moral seemed to be that pilots made better fathers.

We were on a southbound leg of our patrol when the lights at Delmenhorst flashed on for a second and a stream of flak went straight up.

"There's a Jerry around," Sid said.

We crossed the autobahn just west of the field and did a wide circuit around the field. There was some cloud but we could make out a runway.

Again, the lights flashed on for a couple of seconds.

"He's trying to land," Sid said. "Where in hell is he?"

We made another wide sweep. The flak warning to Jerry went up again. There must be more than one Jerry plane getting into position to land. Suddenly, the navigation lights of a plane came on ahead of us.

"Yowie," Sid yelled and pushed the throttles forward. I couldn't believe it. Forty trips and we hadn't seen anything in the air except doodlebugs and our own burning bombers.

Jerry kept his lights on. That was strange. He had been warned there was an intruder about. And we didn't seem to be catching up to it very fast. Sid put on more juice but we couldn't get close enough for a shot.

Suddenly, Sid said, "Look out the back."

I turned around. "Jesus," I said. "There's something up our ass."

I had caught a glimpse of another plane behind us. Sid took what is called violent evasive action. He did things with the Mosquito which the manual said shouldn't be done.

"The dirty bastards," Sid grouched.

The plane ahead of was a decoy while a fighter sneaked up our chuff. The decoy's lights went out. We dropped our speed and resumed our circuit of the field. I kept staring out the back.

"We'll try an old trick," Sid said.

"What old trick?" I asked. The old routine was hard enough on me without any tricks.

"Let's get away from here for a while."

We flew southeast for about twenty miles and stooged around for fifteen minutes. "They'll think we've gone," Sid said.

I gave him the course back to Delmenhorst. As we approached the field, Sid turned on our navigation lights.

"What in hell are you playing at?" I said. We were a flying Christmas tree.

"They'll think we're a Jerry," Sid said. And I was the king of Siam.

A few seconds later, the whole field lit up, perimeter, runway, funnels, the works.

"Now watch for somebody landing." We went around the circuit as if we were a Jerry coming in after a hard night's work of shooting down half a dozen Lancs.

"Jesus, there he is," Sid yelled. We were near the final approach ourselves and the Jerry control tower must have thought he was talking to us.

Jerry didn't have any lights burning but we caught a momentary glimpse of an engine exhaust. We were that close.

Unfortunately, we couldn't pull around in time for a good shot. Sid fired anyway, letting loose the whole works for more than a second.

The lights on the field went off as suddenly as they had come on. Immediately, Sid turned off our lights.

A couple of seconds later, there was a hell of an explosion on the runway and we could see a plane burning. We couldn't tell what kind of plane it was.

"You must have hit him," I said. "He must have run right into our blast."

"No, I missed him by a mile," Sid said. "The son of a bitch panicked."

I could well imagine that. Jerry is moments away from landing, the control tower sees us firing, screams at Jerry that there is an intruder right behind him. Jerry doesn't know whether to land as fast as he can or go around again or put his head in the sand and pray. Instead, he stalls right over the runway.

We're well away from the field by this time.

"I should have been burning nav lights over Germany all the time," Sid said. "Let's go up to that other field and try it again."

"Not twice in one night," I protested. What I meant was, not twice in one tour. I kept turning from right to left checking to see whether the navigation lights at the wingtips were on.

After a while, Sid said, "It wasn't a real great shot."

"You finally got one in the air."

"We probably had nothing to do with it." Sid said. "Maybe it was a trainer on its first night flight."

"Are we going to claim one destroyed?"

"We'll just tell 'em what happened."

"You want a course home?"

"No, give me one back to that field." Sid often could not remember the name of the target. As for me, all the names were written on my forehead.

"What do you want to go back there for?"

"I'm going to put on our lights again and go in and shoot the piss out of their control tower. How would that be for a surprise?"

"That place is a little sore with one of their planes toasting right in the middle of the field," I said. Would this crazy bugger stop trying to win the Victoria Cross?

"Our time's not up." Sid meant we hadn't done a full patrol of two hours yet.

"Yes," I said glumly.

"Well, let's go back to the north field and finish." He meant Lemwerden.

I had to change course from northwest to northeast. We patrolled in what I thought was the right area, allowing lots of room for error to keep us away from Bremen. My map showed the dreaded red for flak for miles around.

It was getting cloudier when we started for home and Sid

had another hour of staring at the artificial horizon, gyro compass, altimeter, and air speed indicator while I kept track of the seconds and minutes.

This might be our last trip, I thought, and Sid had nothing more to show for a tour than a whole lot of stuff blown up on the ground.

He had one more thing to show for it: a grateful navigator. I wasn't in the war to win medals. I was in it to get through it alive. If he was reponsible for my survival, he was the greatest flier ever born or made. After all, what had he been flying all these months except a fragile thing of wood and glue with a starboard seat occupied by young White Knuckles himself?

We got out over the North Sea. I shivered. I took off one shoe and tried to warm up my foot by clutching it with both hands. My socks were so damp I could practically wring them out.

I knew why I was shivering, despite the heavy sweater under my tunic. I had broken out into my usual sweat during our patrol. Besides, this might not be our last trip. Sid right now was probably plotting some long-range daylight foray into Czechoslovàkia or Hungary where some of our guys had already gone — and from where some had not come back.

I didn't dare ask him.

We landed with my fingers grasping the windowledge and the intelligence officer said he thought it would be entirely fitting if we claimed one unidentified enemy aircraft destroyed. We did, but it didn't get into the official record books, which is also fitting, I guess.

We looked at the crew board, as we always did, when we had come into the ops room. Jack and George were still airborne, though they had been due back a few minutes ahead of us.

"Must be having some joy," Sid said.

"Or coming back on one engine," I remarked.

When we finished our report for the IO, Jack and George still weren't back.

Sid picked up the phone and called the control tower. "Anything on three-one?"

The reply was obviously "no" because Sid said, "Please give me a ring when you get something. Yes, the ops room."

"Nothing." Sid took a chair beside mine in front of the dying stove. Everybody else was back.

We were both smoking, as usual. I had never smoked much before I reached the squadron but I was a chainmaster now. At the moment, I was smoking from post-trip relief instead of pre-trip nerves.

"A dumb trip," Sid said.

I didn't think it was so bad.

"I mean Jack's," Sid said. "Bad weather and there's never anything at that field." He was referring to Twente, one of those rotten targets we had taken a turn or two at ourselves.

Sid got up and began scuffing the cigarette butts as he walked around the ops room. He went to the phone again: "Anything on three-one?"

Another ten minutes went by. "Let's go over to the tower," Sid said.

It wasn't far away but I had to turn up my collar against the damp air. It was always damp in this bloody country.

We went up the one flight of narrow cement stairs to the tower. Near the door was the switchboard, which looked like a village telephone exchange, with one girl on duty. The room opened out from there. On the right wall hung the flight board and in the center stretched a ten-yard-long desk covered with transmitters and receivers, maps, and dozens of telephones. Beyond the desk were high, wide windows which looked out on runway two-seven. Because the blackout curtains were open, you had to pause inside the door to allow your eyes to adjust to the darkness. Everything and everybody in the tower presented a faint blue silhouette. I could make out things quite easily once my eyes adjusted and the people working in control moved around in their domain as if it were broad daylight. Joan, the Brit airwoman I knew, was working the switchboard and Bradley was in his accustomed place at the desk.

"Call Manston again," Bradley said.

Joan did so in a second by plugging into the top row on the board in front of her. Manston was the great receptacle for cripples. It is on the North Foreland, the eastern edge of Kent which juts into the English Channel. There the RAF built a base with a multitude of east-west runways to take all the shot-up bombers and fighters struggling back to England, hoping to make land to avoid ditching in the sea. Fire engines and ambulances were parked all over the place all the time. The call sign for Manston was Manlove.

"This is Grapeshot," Joan said. "Do you have three-one?"

"Nothing," she told Bradley.

"Try Coltishall," Gravel Voice said.

"I already . . . " she started to say.

"Try it again."

She plugged in and again reported: "Nothing."

The flying control officer got up from his chair, walked around the ops desk and stood in front of the windows, staring out into the gloom. I think he had seen Sid and me standing near the door but he didn't say anything.

"Where in hell is three-one?" said Bradley, lighting another cigarette from the one in his mouth. He was addressing the airdrome spread out in front of him with its little pinpricks of amber and blue lights.

"Never known three-one to be late yet," said Gravel Voice. "What's he doing, anyway?" There was no reply, of course, from the five others on duty in the tower or from us.

There was a long silence except for the incessant buzzing of the VHF receiver.

A light lit up on the switchboard and we all waited expectantly. But it was the IO in the ops room wanting to know if the tower had anything on three-one.

"I suppose he wants to get home to bed," said Bradley. He waved toward the switchboard. "Call Sector."

Nothing yet.

"Keep calling every five minutes," Bradley said.

I looked at the clock. It was three minutes to three.

Sid and I found chairs out of the way. We continued smoking, without saying anything.

Bradley said to the sergeant: "Maybe their wireless packed up and they'll be giving us a flare any minute. Get a man outside ready to give them a green flare." That meant they could come straight in.

The sergeant made a telephone call. Bradley paced up and down in front of the windows. Once in a while, he stepped outside onto the cement balcony so that he could get a better view, of what we didn't know.

"It's getting late," Sid noted.

"Yes."

It was all we'd said.

"Why are you guys here?" Bradley asked suddenly. It was silly. He knew perfectly well why we were there.

"Just so we could get any word right away," I said needlessly.

"Yes, of course." He turned to Joan: "Call Sector." Sector was our control for one piece of Fighter Command. It was 0301.

Again nothing.

"They've been putting out a call for three-one," she told Bradley.

Fifty-two minutes overdue. Well, it was still possible if Jack had lost an engine at the far end of his run. But his target hadn't been that deep.

The FCO said "Damn, damn," and returned to his chair. This seemed to be a sign that he had given up on three-one. Instead, he ordered another round of phone calls to every station he could think of, though he was supposed to deal with sector control.

There was no complaint from the five others on duty. Gravel Voice cared. And if he cared, by God, everybody was going to care.

The light for the ops room came up on the switch-board.

"They're closing down," Joan reported to Bradley.

A few minutes later, the truck went by with the IO and whomever else was left there.

Another switchboard light came on.

"No I guess not," Joan said. "Cookie wants to know whether there is anybody wanting to eat," she said to me. "He has two pieces of liver and two eggs left."

Bradley sank deeper into his chair, one hand over his eyes. Sid and I sat smoking, watching the clock hands go around.

It was getting on to 0400 when Bradley finally stirred. "Sergeant, you and the others go home. And tell the man with the flare to go home. I'll stay."

Somebody always had to be on duty whether the squadron was flying or not.

"I'll stay," said the sergeant.

"Go," said Bradley.

Joan took off her headset and started to put on her coat. Sid and I got up.

"Sorry," said Bradley. He said it as if it were all his fault that Jack and George hadn't come back.

Sid and I didn't say anything. We followed Joan out the door and down the stairs. We'd ride in the same truck as the control tower crew.

On the stairs, I saw that Joan was crying. She wasn't making any sound but the tears were running down her face.

"I didn't know you knew Jack and George," I said. Past tense already.

"I didn't." Perhaps she cried for every missing crew, I thought. "It's Bradley," she said.

I could visualize him slumped there, the dawn creeping in, the receiver buzzing, buzzing, but conveying no information.

I slept well and the next morning I realized that as much

as I'd liked Jack and George, my attitude was unchanged: better them than us.

Sid and I didn't mention the subject. We didn't even say maybe they're POWs. It sometimes happened that a crew got down safely and was taken prisoner, but that was a small minority of the missing. We were just running true to form. The missing were seldom mentioned. It was like football players who can't bear to watch an injured teammate on the field. Not discussing the missing was putting out of mind all thought that you might go missing yourself. The barriers to memory went up automatically when a friend disappeared.

That afternoon, we were informed that the squadron was moving to Hartford Bridge in a few days.

We did a night flying test in preparation for operation forty-two on November 15. The weather was bad and we were scrubbed. We did another NFT November 16. The weather was bad again, praise be. I spent nearly every waking moment looking out the window, hoping it would never clear.

The day it cleared, we moved to Hartford Bridge. We made a final, low pass at Hunsdon, and Sid nearly hit the flagpole. Ha, ha. We get through forty-one trips and he almost wraps us, literally, in the Union Jack.

I flew back to Hundson in the afternoon with Morey in the Oxford to pick up another load of baggage. Morey was half cut and giggled all the way. His flying was OK, as far as I could see, but I appreciated more than ever that Sid was no boozer.

When we got back to the new station, I found Sid in the mess. "I've got news for you, boy," he said.

Did I dare hope?

"We're screened."

Glory be to God, operation forty-one was the last.

I saw Russ at the bar and rushed over to him, grabbed his hand and started pumping it up and down. "Thanks a million," I gabbled.

Russ had probably never seen relief etched so indelibly on one face.

Sid said to me, "Don't paw him."

"Well, my God, will you look who's here." I hadn't noticed the man standing beside Russ at the bar. He really did look startled to see us.

He was a big man. Group Captain Mitchell had been our chief flying instructor at High Ercall. He looked at Sid and me in continued amazement. "If ever there were two men I never expected to see again, it's you two," he said. "I could have sworn you'd never get through a tour."

"Well, the navigation wasn't much, but the flying was everything you taught me," Sid said.

They went on chatting, but I didn't hear. I was buying triples for Russ and Sid and me and even Mitchell, who was killed a few weeks later on his fourth tour.

EPILOGUE

Sid volunteered our services, without asking me, for the Pacific war. He confided that this would provide a fast way of getting home. It did. We were home for Christmas, 1944. All I remember about the trip on the Queen Mary is that I played bridge with a guy for three days before I noticed his ears had been burned off.

We were both awarded the Distinguished Flying Cross, an honor shared by only 4,000 other Canadian aircrew officers. The citation for mine said I had shown "great skill and determination in navigating his pilot to the target and back." If they measured determination by efforts to get your mouth closed after it had fallen open in fright, I was their man.

Sid's citation said his "outstanding record" had been "an inspiration to all his squadron."

The official history of the RCAF overseas, vol. III, page 322, says: "His score with Hitler was now settled."

You can look it up if you don't believe me.

A later RCAF history of 418 squadron described Sid as

an "operational pilot whose eagerness to attack the enemy has known no bounds."

They had the grace not to attribute similar eagerness to me.

Sid and I never flew together again. He instructed pilots at Debert, Nova Scotia. I tried to teach some navigators at Greenwood, Nova Scotia. I went to San Francisco to see Sid when the war ended and blew every penny to my name in ten days. It was worth every cent of it. War is great for the survivors.

When I was working in Vancouver in 1951, my wife and I went to San Francisco on vacation. Sid simply moved out of his apartment and gave it to us while we were in town.

I never saw him again. We continued to correspond, but he was always in places like Sierra Leone and the Caroline Islands.

He was working in the Palau Islands, part of the Carolines in the far western Pacific, when, on December 6, 1965, he was asked to search for three men missing in a boat. He took off that morning in his own plane. He was never seen again. On December 14 the three missing men were picked up by a fishing vessel. They were tired, sunburnt, but well.

Canadian Memories

A new series on Canada's heroic heritage

YEARS OF SORROW, YEARS OF SHAME
The Story of the Japanese Canadians
in World War II
by Barry Broadfoot

The dramatic story of how the Canadian government reacted to Pearl Harbor and moved the entire Japanese population to points 'East of the Rockies'. It was a terrible time, often shocking, often heart-breaking. The interviews with the survivors are frightening and we should not forget what happened.

TEN LOST YEARS 1929-1939
Memories of Canadians Who
Survived the Depression
by Barry Broadfoot

The Depression — as all its survivors know — was a time when unbelievable things happened regularly. This book is a picture of greed and heroism, a grassroots story that still affects Canadians today.

SIX WAR YEARS 1939-1945
Memories of Canadians at Home and Abroad
by Barry Broadfoot

"Six War Years . . . is gamy, frank and funny and captures the spirit of the war years, the taste of combat, and the interrelations of people living in a hothouse atmosphere better than any book yet written about Canada's war."
J. L. Granatstein

WARPATH
Canadian Troops Participation in the
Liberation of Europe
by Major G. L. Cassidy, D.S.O.

A gripping, firsthand account of the heroic role played by Canadian soldiers from Normandy to Holland. Major Cassidy describes the tactics and the vicious encounters with the German Seventh Army in the final bloody campaign.

OPERATION FISH
The Amazing Story of How Canada Received and Hid Europe's Gold
by Alfred Draper

The most extraordinary untold story of how the gold of Britain, Holland, Norway and France was brought to Canada for safekeeping and secretly stored in Montreal and Ottawa. This wartime operation was so cloaked in secrecy that few knew of its existence . . . and no one told!

MOSQUITO
Canada's Unique Fighter Plane
by Joe Holliday

The dramatic account of the plywood wonder built by de Havilland of Canada, the men who built them, and those who flew them over Europe in a heroic quest for air supremacy. A true Canadian success story.

50 NORTH
Firsthand Stories of the War From Canada's Atlantic
by Alan Easton

For most of World War II a deadly game of search and destroy was played in the North Atlantic between Hitler's U-boats and Allied convoy escorts. When the unseen enemy struck from below, corvettes, frigates and destroyers saturated the area with tons of deadly, explosive charges.

— — — — — — **ORDER FORM** — — — — — —

Now Get These RICHARD ROHMER Best Sellers!